REVIEW COPY

NOTE TO REVIEWER:

Please credit publisher in your review.

THE NEGRO

Saunders Redding

Publication date:

September 28, 1967

POTOMAC BOOKS, INC. PUBLISHERS

1518 K Street, N.W. Washington, D.C. 20005 347-2620

PLEASE SEND US TWO COPIES OF YOUR REVIEW

The U.S.A. Survey Series

▼

THE NEGRO

The U.S.A. Survey Series

▼

*These concise surveys have a two-fold purpose. Each
book in the series will present Americans with a clear
interpretation of their own country and its traditions, as
well as provide foreign readers with informative, realistic
appraisals of contemporary life in the United States.*

The Farmer by Wheeler McMillen

Education by Joseph F. Kauffman

The Making of Foreign Policy by Andrew H. Berding

Community Development by Richard W. Poston

Cooperatives by Jerry Voorhis

Civil Liberties by Irving Dilliard

The Negro by Saunders Redding

other titles in preparation

POTOMAC BOOKS, INC. PUBLISHERS
1518 K Street, N.W.
Washington, D. C. 20005

THE NEGRO

by

SAUNDERS REDDING

WASHINGTON, D. C.

POTOMAC BOOKS, INC. PUBLISHERS

1967

Printed and bound in the United States of America
by Baird-Ward Printing Company, Inc.
Nashville, Tennessee

Library of Congress Catalogue Card Number 66-19024

Prefatory Note

THE purpose of this book is to trace in historical sequence, but in topical outline, one of the major issues in American life. Presently it is an issue affected by and reflected in almost every substantive policy and practice of government. It helps determine the choice of candidates for local public office and what their expressed attitudes will be once office is attained. More frequently than any other issue, it occupies the attention of the national Congress, and of the executive and judicial branches of government. With African and Asian nations—the darker peoples of the world—forming an increasingly powerful bloc in the United Nations, the issue of bi-racialism versus racial equality fixes the posture of the United States *vis-à-vis* the rest of the world.

The history of this issue in America is not difficult to trace, but the story of the successive and consequential crises it has brought in the United States is, and the whole telling would require a much lengthier book than this. So only that part of the story that defines the Negro's role in it is attempted here. In substance, it is not only the story of a people. It is as well the story of the growth of American democracy—the principles that support it, the idealism that inspires it, and the categorical imperatives that control its options.

The Negro's Contribution to Democracy

Mural by Charles W. White at Hampton Institute, Hampton, Virginia. Photograph for illustration courtesy of Reuben Burrell

THE NEGRO'S CONTRIBUTION TO DEMOCRACY, formally presented to Hampton Institute in 1943, depicts those heroes of Negro history who have fought against anti-democratic forces, symbolized by the figure in the background who clutches laborers and machinery, the means of production; and by the Colonial Tory in the lower left-hand corner who destroys a bill by which the Provincial Congress, in 1775, sought to outlaw the sale or importation of slaves in America.

Negro heroes shown fighting against undemocratic elements are: Crispus Attucks, falling before the guns of the redcoats in the Boston Massacre; behind them, Peter Salem, who killed Major Pitcairn of the British army at the Battle of Bunker Hill; and Nat Turner, with flaming torch, and Denmark Vesey, on horseback, who led armed revolts against slavery before Emancipation. The angel with the sword represents the religious mysticism by which they were inspired. Bearded Frederick Douglass is shown with the Negro soldiers whom he persuaded Abraham Lincoln to utilize in the Civil War.

In the upper right-hand portion of the mural, beneath the arch symbolizing the Underground Railway, Sojourner Truth beckons to freedom-loving slaves. Beyond her are Harriet Tubman, an ardent underground worker, and Peter Still, who waves his immortal declaration: "I will die before I submit to the yoke."

In the right foreground are Booker T. Washington, George Washington Carver in his laboratory, Marian Anderson, Ferdinand Smith, Paul Robeson, and Leadbelly, with guitar. The figures in the center foreground represent the contemporary Negro family. The young man holds a blueprint, symbolizing the planned society, free of social wrongs, for which the Negro fights today.

Marchers on Constitution Avenue approach Lincoln Memorial and culmination of massive civil rights rally in Washington, D.C.

Cover and jacket photographs also show groups participating in the "March on Washington," August 28, 1963.

Contents

Prefatory Note vii

PART I. THE HOUSE OF BONDAGE, 1619-1865 1

Chapter One. THE NEGRO IN THE NEW WORLD 3

    1. Indentureship and Slavery 3
    2. Rebellion and Control 5

Chapter Two. THE CONSCIENCE OF THE COUNTRY 11

    1. The Letter and the Spirit 11
    2. The Bond and the Free 13
    3. The Slavery Controversy 14
    4. The "House Divided" 17

Chapter Three. THE CIVIL WAR 19

PART II. OH, FREEDOM, 1865-1918 23

Chapter Four. RECONSTRUCTION AND THE
POLITICS OF RACE 25

    1. Negro "Domination" and Negro "Equality" 25
    2. The White Man's Pattern and the
       Black Man's Place 28
    3. Separate and Unequal 30
    4. The Great Debate: B. T. Washington
       and W. E. B. DuBois 33

Chapter Five. PEOPLE ON THE MOVE 37

    1. The NAACP and the Urban League 38
    2. The Race Problem Moves North 40
    3. World War 42

PART III. THE CHALLENGE OF DEMOCRACY, 1918-1954 .. 45

Chapter Six.   "PEACE" AND THE "RETURN TO
NORMALCY" 47

    1. The Swing Toward the Right 47
    2. The "New Negro"and the Old Problems 49
    3. Creative Expression 51

Chapter Seven.   DEPRESSION, NEW DEAL, AND
WORLD WAR II 55

    1. Programs and Prospects 56
    2. The Continuing Challenge 58
    3. Advances and Advantages 59
    4. New Perspectives and New Power 62

PART IV. "THE UNIVERSAL DECLARATION OF HUMAN
RIGHTS," 1954-1967 67

Chapter Eight.   THE NEW NEGRO SELF-IMAGE 69

    1. New Tactics 71
    2. The Negro Revolution 74
    3. "Adequately and Fairly" 80

Suggestions for Further Reading 91
Index 95

PART I

THE HOUSE OF
BONDAGE, 1619-1865

Chapter One

THE NEGRO IN THE NEW WORLD

ALTHOUGH at first the English settlers in the new world kept only the sketchiest records of their colonial enterprise, one event has always been beyond dispute. In 1619, a ship flying a Dutch flag put in at Jamestown, a settlement in Virginia, and discharged a cargo of twenty Negroes. These were not the first Negroes in the new world. One, Pedro Alonzo, was captain of Columbus' ship, the *Nina*. There were Negroes with Balboa in the Pacific, and with Ponce de Leon in Florida, and a black man named Estevanico explored the Southwest and was killed by the Zuni Indians. But the Negroes who were landed at Jamestown were the first of unwilling thousands for whom America would be home.

Indentureship and Slavery

The English colonists did not immediately impose upon these black people a condition of absolute slavery. Under a system of bondage called indentureship, which operated for imported whites as well, Negroes were bound to service for a term of years, which seldom exceeded fourteen. If a servant committed a crime or failed to give satisfaction, the period of indentureship could be extended; but once it was over, the servant was freed and granted "head rights", which entitled him to take up land of his own. The records indicate that this was the pattern and the practice for almost fifty years. Although there were a few slaves *durante vita* as early as 1640, perpetual slavery had no legal status in Virginia, nor anywhere in the American colonies, until 1661.

But when it did acquire such status, perpetual slavery

meant Negro slavery. Because they were heathen, Negroes could not claim the white Christian's immunity to perpetual bondage. Indeed, in 1667, the Virginia legislature decreed that the "baptism [of a Negro] does not alter the condition . . . as to his bondage." Moreover, it was an advantage for masters to have slaves of a race not their own. It put the slaves beyond any protective considerations of consanguinity. Being "different", if they committed offenses, they could be punished with fewer qualms. Because they were highly visible, if they ran away, they could the more easily be caught. Their blackness was said to be the mark of Cain.

This was one of the rationalizations of a situation that was not easy to live with. From the beginning, there were those who protested that slavery was contrary to Christian principles. Scotch Presbyterians and Irish Protestants in Virginia and Carolina opposed it. In Pennsylvania, the Quakers, then a new sect, organized classes for the religious instruction of slaves and free Negroes, and were instrumental in promoting laws to hamper and finally to prohibit the importation of slaves. But in 1712, the British Parliament declared such statutes inoperative—an action that later led Thomas Jefferson to accuse the Crown of "violating the most sacred right of life and liberty of a distant peoples . . . captivating them into slavery in another hemisphere. . . ."

Jefferson's concern was not only moral and pietistic. It was ideological as well. Some half century after the death of John Locke, the ideas of that English philosopher began to fire men's minds across the Atlantic. They were ideas having to do with the natural rights of man, and with man's place in a rational scheme of things, and with man's inherent dignity. They were ideas that emphasized "natural law", which was incompatible to slavery, and they were finding expression in the writing of James Otis and Thomas Paine, and in the growing spirit of rebellion among the American colonists.

And Jefferson's concern was also economic and social, though he was not the first to realize that slave labor tended to demoralize and debase free white labor, nor the first to take alarm at the "bloody scenes" that were enacted from time to time.

Rebellion and Control

For slaves, too, felt rebellious, and occasionally gave play to the feeling. Indeed, as far back as 1672, the Virginia assembly had found it necessary to warn the colony that "it hath been manifested. . . that many negroes have lately been, and are now out in rebellion in sundry parts of this country, and that noe means have yet been found for the apprehension and suppression of them from whom many mischiefes of very dangerous consequences may arise to the country if either other negroes, Indians or servants should happen to fly forth and joyne them."

Beginning with the eighteenth century, slave rebellions occurred, and slave conspiracies to rebel were uncovered with frightening regularity. Rebellious slaves in New York City made the year 1712 memorable by setting fires and killing the whites who rushed forth to quench the flames. In 1739, Cato, a slave in South Carolina, led more than a hundred slaves in an attempt to fight their way to Florida, where the governor of that Spanish colony had promised freedom to all fugitive slaves. Only ten slaves made it, but Cato's band had set an example of terrible violence. Maryland, Virginia, the Carolinas, and Georgia were kept in a state of alarm. More than one traveler through the South noted that "every white man was a soldier" and "every town an armed camp". Following the long, bloody, and finally successful slave revolt in Haiti in 1791-93, Thomas Jefferson wrote to the governor of South Carolina: "It is high time we should foresee the bloody scenes which our children cer-

tainly, and possibly ourselves (south of the Potomac), have
to wade through, and try to avert them."

Less striking, though far more widespread, were cases of
individual rebellion and vengeance. Acting alone, slaves de-
liberately damaged tools, disabled work horses and mules,
poisoned wells. They committed thefts—often of food to
supplement their inadequate and monotonous diet—sometimes of valuable articles which they buried or destroyed.
They set fire to barns and ruined stored crops by other means.
Hundreds of slaves murdered their masters. But, ordinarily,
slaves rebelled by running away. Many, of course, were re-
captured, but many made good their escape. The newspapers were full of advertisements for runaway slaves. Running
away was so prevalent that a new profession—the "nigger
hunter"—and a new breed of dog—the "nigger hound"—de-
veloped.

But there were other means to control slaves. Militarism,
already mentioned, was general. Every slave-holding state
had its militia, as well as voluntary military units. Each
plantation district was patrolled by armed men, especially at
night, and it was their duty to stop and question any Negro
found unaccompanied by a white person on the public
roads. If the Negro refused to halt on command, or if he
resisted, he could be killed with impunity. Plantation overseers—a class of men noted for their oppressive cruelty—
went armed with gun and whip, and their authority over
the slaves was seldom questioned. In most instances, the
wages overseers earned depended upon the amount of labor
they could wring from their charges. It was practically a
rule of thumb to work an adult slave to death in a few
years and buy another. Cruelty, which was as basic to the
slave system as water is to life, was sanctioned by law.

In 1741, a justice of the North Carolina Supreme Court
declared that "the power of the master must be absolute to
render the submission of the slave perfect"; and more than

a century later, in 1847, the Constitutional Court of South Carolina ruled that: "A slave can invoke neither Magna Charta nor common law. . . . In the very nature of things he is subject to despotism. Law to him is only a compact between his rulers, and the questions which concern him are matters agitated between them. The various acts concerning slaves contemplate throughout the subordination of the servile class to every free white person and enforce the stern policy which the relation of master and slave necessarily requires. Any conduct of a slave inconsistent with due subordination contravenes the purpose of these acts."

That was the spirit around which congregated a rigid body of law and custom called Black Codes. Under these codes, slaves had no rights, no redress. They could be whipped, branded, have their noses slit and their ears cropped for behavior offensive to their masters. A white man was not liable to prosecution for killing a slave, unless the slave were not his own, in which case he was required to make restitution. Slaves were forbidden to defend themselves from assault by whites. They could not testify against white persons. They could not sue or be sued, own property, nor buy, sell, or trade. Their marriages had no legal status. In short, slaves were chattels.

But all this was troubling to the American conscience. All of it was persistently challenged by the political philosphy and the humanitarian ideas that grew ever more clangorous in the land. Slavery simply could not be reconciled to the new revolutionary sentiments, though there were those who tried to reconcile them. Most thoughtful Americans, however, saw the inconsistency of petitioning for those "inalienable rights" that they denied to others. Southern aristocrats, like Thomas Jefferson of Virginia, and Henry Laurens of South Carolina, were deeply troubled. Patrick Henry, another Southerner who was to become famous as a patriot, wrote a friend in the North: "Is it not amazing, that at a time when the rights of Humanity are defined and understood with precision in a Country above all others fond of Liberty; that in such an Age and such a Country, we find Men, professing a Religion the most humane, mild, meek, gentle and generous, adopting a Principle as repugnant to humanity. . . . Would anyone believe that I am Master of Slaves of my own purchase!"

Those who held these sentiments inevitably saw the issue of slavery as conjoined with the issue of British domination. From the beginning of revolutionary agitation, even some Negroes understood this, and how their interests were involved. Not all of them were ignorant. Some, particularly in the middle colonies, had the benefit of attending classes set up for them by the Quakers and members of the Society for the Propagation of the Gospel. The Quakers were also active anti-slavery propagandists. In June, 1775, members of this sect presented a resolution to the Massachusetts Committee of Correspondence which declared: "We abhor the enslaving of any of the human race, and particularly of the Negroes in this country and that whenever there shall be. . . [an] opportunity present for anything to be done towards the emancipation of Negroes, we will use our influence and endeavor that such a thing may be brought about."

But, indeed, as early as 1661, Negroes were themselves petitioning for freedom, and when the revolutionary fervor began to intensify, following the passage of the Sugar Act in 1764, their petitions seldom failed to tie in their aims with the aims of the quickening struggle against "foreign domination". "In imitation of the Laudable Example of the Good People of these States", a group of slaves addressed the House of Representatives of the State of Massachusetts Bay, "your petitioners have Long and Patiently waited the Event of petition after petition By them presented to the Legislative Body of this state and cannot but with Grief Reflect that their Success hath been but too similar they Cannot but

express their Astonishment that It have never Bin Con-
sirdered that Every Principle from which Amarica has Acted
in the Cours of their unhappy Dificultes with Great Briton
Pleads Stronger than A thousand arguments in favours of
your petioners they therfor humble Beseech your honours to
give this petion its due weight & consideration & cause an
act of the Legislatur to be past Wherby they may be Restored to the Enjoyments of that which is the Naturel Right
of all men. . . ."

When the war with England came in 1775, and Lord Dun-
more, the Royal Governor of Virginia, promised freedom to
all Negroes who went over to the British, the issue of Negro
freedom and the issue of American independence were con-
cretely joined. The following year, General George Washington reversed his policy of not enlisting Negroes in the
Continental Army, and, in July, the Continental Congress issued the Declaration of Independence, which, though it did
not refer specifically to slavery, proclaimed that "all men are
created equal and are endowed with certain inalienable
rights", among them liberty. Eventually all the states except
South Carolina and Georgia promised freedom to Negroes
who joined the state militia, and the Continental Congress
offered to pay owners of slaves up to $1000 for each able-
bodied Negro who enlisted in the army.

While thousands of Negro slaves escaped to the British
lines (and were subsequently evacuated over the protest of
George Washington), approximately five thousand Negroes
fought for American independence. They fought at Bunker
Hill, Valley Forge and Brandywine, Saratoga and Savannah,
Trenton and Yorktown; and they were on the ships that
defended American waters from Virginia to the Gulf.

Chapter Two

THE CONSCIENCE OF THE COUNTRY

THE American Revolution—its slogans, its objects and its deeds—created a climate that encouraged the spread of anti-slavery sentiment. Although there was no coordination of effort until the last decade of the eighteenth century, abolition societies sprang up in all the states from Virginia to Massachusetts, and there was anti-slavery activity as far south as Georgia.

The Letter and The Spirit

It was a time of stern denunciations of the "iniquitous institution" and of ringing declarations for the "natural rights of man". The arguments against slavery were posited on various grounds, social, moral, and religious. Methodists and Baptists were as eloquent and vigorous as Quakers in opposing human bondage. On the other hand, Catholics and Anglicans seemed generally to accommodate it, although George Mason, a native Virginian and an outstanding layman in the Episcopal church, declared that "slavery discourages arts and manufactures. The poor despise labor when performed by slaves. . . [who] produce the most pernicious effect on manners. Every master of slaves is born a petty tyrant. They bring the judgment of heaven on a Country. . . . By an inevitable chain of causes and effects providence punishes national sins by national calamities."

When the Constitutional Convention met in 1787, Benjamin Franklin, chief delegate from Pennsylvania, was deputized by the Pennsylvania Society for the Abolition of Slavery to submit a resolution opposing the institution; but, if

11

an opportune moment to do this presented itself, Franklin
failed to take advantage of it. The Convention hassled over
questions that in the circumstances seemed more important
than slavery *per se:* constituent branches of government
and the division of responsibilities among them; the rights
of the states and the composition of the Congress; taxation
and proportional representation.

This latter question did stimulate a discussion of slavery
that ran through several sessions, but it was largely tangen-
tial. The issue was whether slaves should be counted in the
population for purposes of congressional apportionment.
Delegates from the North said no. The South, where slaves
were chattels, said an ironic yes, and went on to defend
slavery on economic grounds. Slavery, the southern delegates said, was in "the interest of the whole Union. The more
slaves, the more produce to employ the carrying trade; the
more consumption also, and the more of this, the more of
revenue for the common treasury." A compromise was
struck. The document that was finally hammered out during
four months of debate provided, among other things, that
slaves should be counted "three-fifths of all other persons".

But the Southerners' economic argument for slavery was
certainly debatable at the time. Slavery, the slave-market,
and slave-produced crops such as cotton, tobacco, rice, and
indigo were in acute depression. "Prime slaves" were selling
for piddling sums. "Healthy female slaves, capable of child-
bearing" were a drug on the market even at a top price of
$300. England, the chief outlet for cotton and tobacco, was
importing little of either. Moreover, slavery had already
proved an economic failure in the Caribbean. The bloodiest
slave rebellion of modern times raged in Santo Domingo in
1791. This was terrible proof that slavery was a social failure,
too.

But in that very year, the American industrial revolution
got under way when Samuel Slater opened a spinning mill

in Rhode Island. Eli Whitney's cotton gin was ready in 1793, and, shortly thereafter, the perfection of the steam engine and the increasing use of mechanics in manufacturing began to affect profoundly the economy and the culture of the country and to alter the shape of the American mind. One obvious, immediate result was the transformation of cotton, heretofore a troublesome and barely profitable fiber, into "golden fleece". The cultivation of cotton spread to Georgia and Arkansas, and in 1803, when Louisiana was purchased from France, to the Gulf of Mexico. Meanwhile, the number of American textile mills doubled and tripled, and the hunger of British mills for American cotton grew ever more voracious. The price of cotton, the value of cotton land and of the slaves who worked it zoomed beyond the planters' brightest hopes. The more land, the more cotton; and the more cotton, the more slaves to plant, hoe, and harvest it.

The Bond and The Free

The application of this formula brought about what seemed to be the unstoppable growth of plantation slavery. The number of slaves increased from a half million in 1775 to two million by 1830, and to nearly four million by 1860. The laws that were enacted to control slaves and to protect the institution of slavery were ever more rigid and more rigorously enforced. Nearly everyone in the South—white masters as well as black slaves—was the victim of this rigidity. In a sense, nearly everyone in the South—whites as well as blacks—was enslaved. On the one side, uneasiness; on the other, restiveness, and both were aggravated by currents of anti-slavery sentiment flowing down from the North, and by the presence of free Negroes, whose number had increased appreciably as a result of the American Revolution, and who were highly visible. In 1830, there were 300,000 free Negroes, nearly half in the South. By 1860, there were 500,000. North and South, they congregated in cities—New York, Philadelphia, Baltimore, Charleston, New Orleans—where the vast majority worked as unskilled laborers. A few worked as carpenters, masons, blacksmiths, and the like, and in the service trades as tailors and dressmakers, barbers and hairdressers. A handful were teachers and preachers. Two or three communities could boast a Negro doctor, a dentist, or a lawyer.

Life was not easy for free Negroes. The competition with white labor in the North was keen and sometimes violent, especially after European immigration mounted to flood in the 1840's. In the South, a wall of proscriptions hemmed free Negroes in. They could not travel at will across state and county lines. In some states, after the 1840's, they could not form associations such as clubs and lodges, and other social and charitable organizations. They could not even worship together, except when an authorized white person was present. They could not "hold schools", nor clerk in stores, nor buy or sell such commodities as tobacco, corn, and whisky. They could not vote.

Just the same, they were an embarrassment to the South. Indeed, they were considered a bane. Chancellor Harper of the South Carolina Supreme Court put it this way in 1845: "A free African population is a curse to any country. . . and the evil is exactly proportional to the number of such population. This race, however condusive they are in a state of slavery. . . in a state of freedom and in the midst of a civilized community, are a dead weight to the progress of improvement. . . they become pilferers and marauders, and corrupters of the slaves."

The Slavery Controversy

If many Southern whites agreed with the Chancellor's judgment—and of course many did—it was not because they were villainous or necessarily more inhumane. Rather it was because the slaveholding oligarchy was committed to an order of society, a system of human relationships, a way of life that seemed to them to support the "aristocratic ideals" of luxury, leisure, and accomplishment. Morality was not the issue: civilization, the Southern culture, was; and when the issue of morality was forced on them, they were content with the argument set forth by the president of Randolph-Macon College, an aristocratic Southern institution. "In general," Dr. William A. Smith said, "hired service is in point of fact, as involuntary as slave labor. . . that the abstract principle of the institution of slavery, and the principle of natural rights, coincide, and that both have the unqualified approbation of Holy Scripture, cannot be successfully controverted. Natural rights and the principles of slavery do not conflict."

But when that was written in the 1840's, nearly all the issues that were to lead inevitably to conflict were already defined and already joined, and the men who would argue them most effectively throughout the next twenty years— Clay of Kentucky, Calhoun and Hayne of South Carolina, Jackson and Johnson of Tennessee, Douglas and Lincoln of Illinois, Webster, Sumner, Phillips, and Garrison of Massachusetts, and Frederick Douglass, an ex-slave of Maryland —were already on the national rostrum.

The issues were political, and they involved questions of territories made states and admitted to the Union; of states' rights as against constitutional authority; of the voting power of the South as against the voting power of the North and the newly opening West; of universal white suffrage as against restrictions on the ballot.

The issues were economic, and they involved the recurrent question of tariffs—low in the interest of Southern planters, and high in the interest of Northern industry; state banks and inflation versus a national bank and hard money; federal aid or state aid for highways and railroads, and a Southern or a Northern link to the West.

The issues were social, cultural, and, finally, moral, and

they involved all the questions pertaining to slavery—and these questions cropped up everywhere.

They were at the center of the Missouri Compromise of 1820, which admitted Missouri to the union as a slave-holding state, but prohibited slavery in the territory north of Missouri's southern boundary. They were the questions involved in the compromise of 1850, which, among other things, required the North to return fugitive slaves to the South. They were the theme of *Uncle Tom's Cabin*, published in 1852, and of Abraham Lincoln's response to Stephen Douglas' pro-slavery sentiments in 1858: "A house divided against itself cannot stand. I believe this government cannot endure, permanently half slave and half free." They were the questions that the Supreme Court's Dred Scott decision failed to answer, and that sent John Brown, "God's angry man", to murder slave-holders in Kansas in 1856, and to try rebellion against the slave-holding power in Virginia in 1859.

These were the questions that the abolitionists agitated unceasingly.

When William Lloyd Garrison, in the first issue of his anti-slavery paper, *The Liberator*, declared that he did not "wish to think, to speak, or write with moderation" on the subject of slavery, he established the tone of the anti-slavery debate and the spirit of the abolition movement. It was then evident in 1831 that slavery would not simply wither away. Although schemes for the gradual emancipation and colonization of Negroes had been favored by Thomas Jefferson and President James Monroe, and were later supported by Abraham Lincoln, they had very limited success. A few Negroes consented to colonization in Africa—for that was the price of manumission—and the American Colonization Society helped them to establish the Republic of Liberia. But many Negroes, feeling that the United States was home, opposed African colonization. And anyway, by the 1840's most

Southern states had enacted laws to discourage manumission.

But by that time, too, the abolitionists were in full cry. Their agents fanned out through the country. They proposed legislation and presented petitions in state chambers and in the national Congress. They debated the question of slavery in the press and on the platform, and Negro abolitionists—among them Frederick Douglass and William Wells Brown—carried the agitation against slavery abroad. Abolitionists defied the Fugitive Slave Law and conducted slaves to freedom on the Underground Railroad, which was neither underground nor a railroad, but a chain of hiding places for runaway slaves along the routes to the free states. The abolitionists contributed money to a "treasonable project" proposed by John Brown, a fanatic who hoped to inspire and lead slaves to rebellion. Abolitionists rioted and incited to riot. With the organization of the Republican Party in 1859, the abolitionists seemed to acquire a political structure and a potential of political power.

The "House Divided"

But if the Party was not wholly committed to abolition, its successful presidential candidate in 1860 was certainly no friend of slavery. As a politician, Abraham Lincoln was a nationalist opposed to splitting the union of the states. As a man, he was an idealist who thought slavery an evil. His duty as a politician was in conflict with his duty as an idealist. His inaugural address was conciliatory to the South. He wanted to bring back into the Union the seven states that had already seceded and formed the Confederate States of America. And in an effort to bring them back, Lincoln said, "there needs be no bloodshed or violence; and there shall be none, unless it is forced upon the national authority. The power confided in me will be used to hold, occupy, and possess the property and places belonging to the government. . . ."

Lincoln felt it his duty to preserve the union. Its dismemberment for him, both as politician and idealist, would be a source of agony. But dismemberment had by this time become inevitable. Five weeks after the inaugural, Confederate artillery opened fire on Fort Sumter in Charleston Harbor, and President Lincoln called the "power confided" to him into play. The Civil War had begun.

Chapter Three

THE CIVIL WAR

No one anticipated a long war, and President Lincoln's reluctant refusal to recognize Negro freedom as an issue did not shorten it. His refusal was based on the grim likelihood that any indication that the war was being fought to abolish slavery would bring the border states of Delaware, Maryland, Missouri, and Kentucky in on the side of the Confederacy. Yet certain realities, equally grim, were at work, too. In the first place, Confederate arms won victory after victory during the first fifteen months. The South put her slaves to work in factories and mills, as road menders and fortification builders, as hostlers, wagoners, and cooks in army camps, thereby releasing more Southern whites to bear arms. Thanks to slavery, manpower in the South seemed limitless; and, indeed—although the authorizing act was not passed until near the end of the war—the South discussed enlisting slaves as soldiers and granting them their freedom.

The fact that the Confederacy recognized slavery and freedom as an issue was certainly not lost on Lincoln, yet two years passed before he publicly acknowledged it. Though privately he had agonized over slavery and had wrestled with the idea of emancipation, it was upon the grounds of military necessity that he finally acted. He issued the Emancipation Proclamation. Almost immediately, the fortunes of war began to change and to flow steadily toward the North. The defection of slaves, escaping to Union lines by the thousands, seriously depleted the South's pool of manpower and crippled her industry. Negroes flocked into the Union ranks. Though commanded by white officers, they were organized into separate units, and they were discriminated against in various ways at first. In pay and allowances they received three dollars less per month than white soldiers. When captured, they were liable to be summarily shot or hanged as rebellious slaves. Not until 1864 did the President of the Confederacy, Jefferson Davis, agree to treat captured Negro soldiers as prisoners of war.

Nevertheless, the morale of Negro troops remained high. Nearly 200,000 Negroes volunteered for the Union army, and nearly 30,000 for the Union navy. From the autumn of 1862 until the end of the war, scarcely a land battle or a naval engagement was fought in which Negroes did not play a part. Seventeen colored soldiers and four colored sailors were awarded the Congressional Medal of Honor. More than 68,000 Negroes died in the fighting.

Meanwhile the spirit of the Negro civil population kept rising under the inspiration of a moral crusade that did not slacken. "We shall appeal to the hearts and consciences", a Negro editor admonished; "not to. . . passions and prejudices. . . to [a] sense of right and justice; not to. . . feelings of pity and commiseration. Be active! Be vigilant! Be not discouraged!" But they were not alone in being active and vigilant—they were not the only crusaders. White abolitionists were still of that company; so were philanthropic and religious organizations such as the National Freedmen's Relief Association and the American Missionary Society. As early as 1862, agents of these charitable groups were taking food, clothing, and medical supplies to black refugees behind the Union lines. They set up makeshift schools; they ministered to the Negroes' spiritual needs.

Nor were these private efforts all that Negro morale had to feed on. In the public sector, in the area of civil and legal rights, there were attitudes expressed, commitments made, and laws passed that gave substance to the belief that there was a "change in public sentiment" towards Negroes. "The revolution has begun", declared an editorial in the *Pacific Appeal*, a Negro newspaper. And so it seemed when, in 1862, slaves were emancipated in the District of Columbia, and when in that same year Congress decreed that in the courts of the District there must be no exclusion of witnesses because of race. Two years later, the law was made to apply to every federal court in the land. By 1865, all the Northern states except Indiana had struck down laws barring Negro immigration, and, in Pennsylvania, the Negro's struggle for civil equality had the active support of the Republican Party and hundreds of other whites whose "only interest [was] in seeing justice done."

The conduct of Negroes who bore the Union's arms contributed to the gains in civil life. Ships piloted by Negroes helped make the blockade of Southern ports effective. Negro soldiers of the First South Carolina Volunteers (of the Union army) were such successful scouts and raiders that their commander, Colonel Thomas Wentworth Higginson, reported that they "have been repeatedly under fire . . . and have in every instance come off not only with unblemished honor, but with undisputed triumph. . . .it would have been madness to attempt, with the bravest white troops, what I have successfully accomplished with black ones." Two regiments of Negroes repulsed and drove back in hand-to-hand fighting a Confederate force of 2500 at Milliken's Bend, and Negro soldiers were proclaimed heroes at Olustee in Florida, and at Petersburg in Virginia.

But success did not always attend their arms. A Negro regiment, the 54th Massachusetts, lost 558 men when it was repulsed at Fort Wagner in one of the fiercest battles of the war. Negro soldiers were defeated at Port Hudson on the lower Mississippi. At Fort Pillow, a Union outpost also on the Mississippi, a Confederate force under General Nathan Bedford Forrest captured some three hundred Negro soldiers, "several score" of whom, according to an official report, "were murdered after they had surrendered".

But by the time of this incident, Confederate arms were desperately weak. The "massacre at Pillow" was their last considerable success—if success it can be called. Within a year, Lee, the South's best military officer, surrendered his army to Grant, the North's most successful general. The war was over. The collapse of the Confederacy was a victory for the idea of union, but it was an even greater victory for the Negro cause and the idea of freedom. It was a triumph. Five days after the surrender at Appomattox, this triumph was darkly shadowed by the assassination of President Abraham Lincoln.

PART II

OH, FREEDOM,
1865-1918

Chapter Four

RECONSTRUCTION AND THE POLITICS OF RACE

THE emancipation of nearly four million slaves was a fact that was not easy to absorb, and the tragic death of Lincoln did not make it any easier. Lincoln had been for moderation all along the line. In 1863, he had outlined a policy of post-war reconstruction that was designed to facilitate the South's economic recovery and her reentry into the Union. Under this policy, which excepted only the top Southern leaders, the suffrage would be restored to all who swore allegiance to the Union. When, in any of the Southern states, one-tenth of the citizens who had voted before 1860 had sworn allegiance, a state government would be formed, and when the state government made constitutional provision for the Negroes' freedom, it would be recognized. As President Lincoln saw it, this was a sufficient start toward the healing of the wounds of war.

Negro "Domination" and Negro "Equality"

But Negroes were shocked and hurt by the absence of a provision for their enfranchisement. They had declared through Frederick Douglass, their outstanding leader: "We want the elective franchise in all the states now in the Union, and the same in all such states that may come into the Union hereafter. . . .The highest welfare of this country will be found in erasing from its statute books all enactments in favor or against any class of its people." And if Negroes were shocked, many whites in Lincoln's own party were angered. They argued that the President's policy was too lenient to the Southern states, which should be treated as "conquered provinces", and not liberal enough to the freedmen, who should be given full citizenship rights. Also in the back of the minds of many Republicans, who took into account the minority status of their party, was the thought of the increase of power that would come with Negro enfranchisement. In 1864, these "radicals" had pushed through the Wade-Davis bill, which made the terms for re-entering the Union more stringent; but when, following Lincoln's assassination, Andrew Johnson moved into the White House, he advocated a policy that was essentially the same as the late President's.

Throughout the remaining months of 1865 and the first two months of the next year, Southern states took advantage of this. They enacted new "black codes"—laws so severely limiting the Negroes' freedom as to make a mockery of it. The laws forbade Negroes to vote; forbade them to testify in court, except in cases involving other Negroes; forbade them to preach without a license. With only slight variations from state to state, the laws restricted Negroes to menial occupations, such as farm laborers and domestic servants; established a Negro curfew; and imposed fines or jail terms on Negroes found guilty of "insulting" acts or gestures. In short, the new black codes had the effect of imposing a condition close to slavery, and even the most painstaking efforts of the Freedmen's Bureau, established by Congress to ease the Negroes' transition to freedom, did not modify the result appreciably.

The North reacted to these new measures with bitter indignation. Many people of that section were suddenly repossessed by the fervor that had characterized the abolition movement. They joined with Negroes in demanding that the South be required to live up to the national commitment to democratic equality. Meanwhile, the Radical Republicans, who hated all that the "Old South" stood for politically, had no intention of submitting to control from the White House, or of missing an opportunity to increase their political power. Led by such adamant men as Thaddeus Stevens and Charles Sumner, the Radical Republican Congress first extended the life and broadened the authority of the Freedmen's Bureau, and then, in 1866, passed, over President Johnson's veto, a Civil Rights Bill, which was intended to assure the Negroes' equality with all other citizens. Finally, the same Congress passed the Fourteenth Amendment to the Constitution, and stipulated that any state that failed to ratify it would not be readmitted to the Union. By 1867, the Congress controlled Reconstruction absolutely, and it exercised its authority by disfranchising a majority of southern whites and by securing the eligibility of Negroes for political office and the assumption of civic responsibility.

The results of Radical Reconstruction have been described as "totally disastrous" and "tragic", and Negroes were burdened with the largest share of blame. It is true that most Negroes were ignorant, and some of them venal. But so were some of the whites called Carpetbaggers, who rushed South, and some of those called Scalawags, who were natives of the area. Some of them manipulated Negroes for purposes the Negroes did not always understand. At no time during the several years of so-called "Negro rule" were freedmen in control of any state legislature. At no time were they in charge of political patronage. Not even in Mississippi and North and South Carolina, the three states where their political strength was greatest, was there a time when either the legislative or executive branch of the government was in Negro hands.

If, as voters and office holders on the level of clerks, justices of the peace, sheriffs, and members of the legislature, they sometimes supported iniquitous men and unwise measures, they more frequently stood behind legislation that was forward-looking and equitable. They were for public education and against property qualifications for voting and holding office. They were for the Fifteenth Amendment, which disallowed discrimination on account of race, creed, color, and the former condition of servitude. They were against anti-labor measures that exploited poor whites as well as blacks. In a few instances, Negroes served as prosecuting attorneys; in two instances, as school superintendents; and in one instance, in Louisiana, a Negro served as lieutenant-governor. After reexamining the Reconstruction period recently, C. Vann Woodward, Sterling Professor of History at Yale, remarked on "the success that a people [Negroes] of such meager resources and limited experience enjoyed in producing the number of sober, honest, and capable leaders and public servants they did."

As for those Negroes who were elected to the national Congress between 1869 and 1901—two to the Senate and twenty to the House—most had proved able in other careers. All of them were educated men. Hiram Revels, who took Jefferson Davis' seat in the Senate, had been an effective school teacher following his graduation from Knox College, and was later to be a college president. Robert Smalls, a member of the House from South Carolina, had been the captain of a Union privateer during the Civil War. George H. White, of North Carolina, the last member of his race to win election to Congress until 1928, was a newspaper editor. Although no national legislation originated with Negro Congressmen, their presence was felt and their voices were heard in Washington. James G. Blaine, the Republican presidential candidate in 1884, who worked with some of them and was acquainted with all of them, described them as "studious, earnest, ambitious men, whose public conduct. . . would be honorable to any race."

The White Man's Pattern and The Black Man's Place

But questions of conduct quite aside, Negro officeholders and the Negro franchise itself, supported by the presence of federal troops, were anathema to the white South. And, again, this could not be attributed solely to viciousness. Most whites in the South, and many in the North, truly believed what the Delaware state legislature declared—that "the unmutable laws of God have affixed upon the brow of the white race the ineffaceable stamp of superiority" and that it was their duty as white men to provide "unceasing opposition to making Negroes eligible for public offices, to sit on juries . . . and to any and every measure designed as having the effect to promote the equality of the Negro with the white man in any of the relations of life."

Southern leaders looked upon themselves as the guardians of a way of life that was "humane and civilized" and "in the natural order of things". They saw "Negro rule"—though it was far from that—as a social disaster, and they considered any means to avoid it, or to overthrow it, justified. Since federal laws, with federal troops to enforce them, protected the Negro in his new rights, Southern leaders turned to extra-legal means. They organized, with popular support, secret societies such as the Knights of the White Camelia, the Jay-hawkers, and the Ku Klux Klan, that spread throughout the South terrorizing Negroes and those whites who sympathized with Negroes. A congressional investigation exposed the tactics of these organizations, and Congress moved to suppress them. Nonetheless, their activities continued practically unchecked, and the enemies of racial equality were once more in control in the South.

The success of the Southern reactionaries and the conservative Democrats can be attributed in part to the growing indifference of the North to the Negro's plight. The North had problems and plans of its own, including the pursuit of the economic gains that would flow from financial investments in the South and from developing Southern markets for industrial products. While Northern Republicans successfully propagandized themselves as friends of the freedmen, they no longer needed the Negro vote; and with the death of Charles Sumner in 1874—Thaddeus Stevens had died ten years earlier—there was no voice to alert them to their responsibility to the "party of Lincoln and equal rights". The new watchword was non-interference in the South's civil affairs. The new shibboleth was that the Negro was the South's problem. The election of Rutherford B. Hayes in 1876, and the immediate recall of federal troops from the South were tokens of the North's changing attitude. The South was now free to exert her will, and her will was to suppress the Negro. State constitutions were hastily revised in such ways as to nullify the Negro's vote, or to disfranchise him altogether. Poll taxes were imposed, literacy tests were devised, and election rules were complicated beyond the ability of most Negroes to follow them. And there were always coercion, intimidation, and violence.

Separate and Unequal

Moreover, two key decisions of the U. S. Supreme Court aided and abetted the enemies of equality. In the first instance—*U. S. v. Cruikshank*—the Court held that the Fifteenth Amendment to the Constitution did not guarantee the right to vote, but only the right not to be discriminated against because of race or color. In *Plessy v. Ferguson,* the second instance, the Court decreed that separation of the races in public accommodations and tax-supported facilities was legal, so long as such accommodations and facilities were equal.

By 1895, Negroes were legally disfranchised and segregated everywhere in the South. Indeed, the states of the old Confederacy had created a pattern of race relations for the whole country to follow, and the vast majority of Negroes seemed to fit into it resignedly.

They were not only deprived of their civil rights, but they found it difficult to make a living. Negroes who had

acquired some skills in slavery found them useless in freedom. Carpenters and stonemasons, blacksmiths and wheel-
wrights dug ditches, swept streets, collected garbage, and
hauled nightsoil. But not even these jobs, nor employment
in the service occupations—as domestics, waiters, bellhops,
and porters—were conceded to them. More and more unskilled immigrants—Irish, Italian, Polish, Greek—competed.
Referring specifically to Chicago, which fairly represented
the Negro situation in the North, a journalist pointed out in
1885 that: "The coloured people have lost about every oc-
cupation that was regarded as peculiarly their own . . . .
When the hordes of foreign folk began to pour into Chicago,
the demand for the Negroes' places began. . . ."

In the South, where more than eighty-five percent of the
Negroes lived, employment in textile and tobacco factories,
as well as in other industries, was the special preserve of
the landless poor whites. Relatively few Negroes managed
to make a living in Southern cities, and Negro men were
especially hard put. Most were relegated to farm labor, usually under a system of share-cropping that tended to degenerate into peonage. In the South fewer than 200,000 of
the 4,500,000 Negroes owned farms in 1890, and the average
acreage for a man with two or more dependents was somewhat below the subsistence level. So even farm owners were
sometimes forced to work for others at wages that seldom
exceeded ten dollars a month.

North and South, schools for Negroes were few and inferior, opportunities were severely limited, and aspirations
were pathetically low. Segregated and discriminated against
in "all the relations of life", Negroes were also politically
powerless. They knew no effective way to lower the barriers
set up in the North. They had no means of breaking out of
the pattern established in a South that was solidified by its
one-party system, its adherence to the tenets of "states'
rights", by its commitment to the myth of "a cause glo-

riously defended and nobly lost", and solidified not least by
an inflexible will "to keep the Negro in his place". For the
Negro, freedom was a legal reality, but second-class citizenship, often bordering on serfdom, was a literal fact.

Nevertheless, resignation was not the Negro people's only
response to their condition. They were restive and restless.
Although centers of Negro sub-culture could be found in
such Southern cities as Atlanta and Savannah, Charleston
and New Orleans, in the 80's and 90's many thousands of
Negroes moved West to Oklahoma, Kansas, Texas, and Cal-
ifornia, while others went North to the industrial sections of
Pennsylvania, Ohio, and Illinois. Fortunately, the Negro
church had survived the social disorganization of the post-
Reconstruction years, and they took the church with them.
It was the one totem around which nearly all Negroes gathered, and now it was put to more than a spiritual use. The
church undertook welfare activities, such as caring for the
indigent aged, setting up employment bureaus, and support-
ing "shelters" for working girls. Negro "academies", "colleges", and "universities", including two or three in the
North, hummed with energy under the aegis of the church.
The quality of these institutions left much to be desired,
but by the beginning of the 20th century, they had gradu-
ated approximately 7500 young men and women who had
become teachers, preachers, physicians, and editors.

And in spite of the North's general indifference to the
race problem, and the South's barricade of laws designed
"to keep the Negro in his place", the Negro got support in
his struggle. There was still a root body of attitudes that
would not die. A social conscience was still at work, and it
was expressed in the philanthropic endeavors of white organizations and individuals. Indeed, the years between 1890
and 1915 were a kind of golden age of private philanthropy.
The American Missionary Association, the Baptist Home
Mission Society, the Presbyterian Board, and the Episcopal

Church recruited teachers and other qualified personnel and sent them South to work among Negroes. Men of great wealth—among them Collis Huntington, John F. Slater, Andrew Carnegie, George Peabody, and John D. Rockefeller—endowed Negro clinics, hospitals, and orphanages. They gave money to such colleges as Talladega and Atlanta Baptist, Tuskegee, Hampton, and Fisk—all of them, except Tuskegee, supervised and largely staffed by whites.

Whether or not with an intent that was wholly conscious, all but two of these institutions aimed at integrating Negroes into middle-class American life. The education they offered was in the standard humanities courses, the liberal arts, and sciences. But humanistic studies struck some as unrealistic and impractical for an impoverished people, whose opportunities to employ "book learning" were severly limited. This was the thinking of Samuel Chapman Armstrong, once an officer in the Union army, who founded Hampton Institute. He had inspired in his students an almost obsessive belief that the only worthwhile education for Negroes was in the manual arts. One of General Armstrong's students was Booker T. Washington, and this man was chosen principal of Tuskegee Institute in 1881.

The Great Debate: B. T. Washington and DuBois

Born in slavery, Booker Washington had lived all of his life in the South, and he prided himself on knowing it. He also prided himself on being practical, and the overriding practical factors in the Southern situation, as he saw it, were the inviolate power and authority of the whites, and the low potential of the Negroes. Under the rubric of "racial inequality", Washington proposed that Negroes make themselves satisfied with second-class citizenship, and in this status become indispensable to the white economic and social structure. "The agitation of questions of social equality is the extremist folly," he declared. He admonished Negroes to have nothing to do with organized labor. They should work "without strikes and labor wars", so the white South could rest assured that it would be "surrounded by the most patient, faithful, law-abiding and unresentful people that the world has ever seen."

When Washington spoke before a large and influential gathering of white people at the Atlanta Exposition in 1895, these sentiments were hailed as the "distillation" of wisdom. They brought joy to the South, for they "heralded a new day", and they pleased those in the North—by far the majority—who, knowing little about the race problem, except that it had been troublesome, wanted to be done with the whole thing. Washington's Atlanta Exposition speech made him *the* Negro leader. For nearly twenty years, no economic, political, or social question affecting Negroes was resolved except on the sought-for advice of Booker Washington.

But there were those Negroes who challenged Washington's opinions and the position of leadership to which whites had lifted him. They were concerned that the dominance of Washington's ideas and the pursuit of his program offended and weakened the equalitarian doctrine upon which American democracy rested. Led by W. E. B. DuBois, a brilliant young social historian, who—thanks to hard work and the encouragement of Northern philanthropy—had been educated at Fisk, the University of Berlin, and Harvard, the group of dissident intellectuals met in Niagara Falls in 1905, and publicly questioned the *status quo*. They demanded, among other things, the restoration of Negro voting rights, the abolition of all distinctions based on race, and a recognition of the principle of the brotherhood of man.

"Never before in the modern age," the Niagara declaration stated, "has a great and civilized folk threatened to adopt so cowardly a creed in the treatment of its fellow-citizens, born and bred on its soil. Stripped of verbose subterfuge and in its naked nastiness, the new American creed says: fear to let black men even try to rise lest they become the equals of the white. And this in the land that professes to follow Jesus Christ. The blasphemy of such a course is only matched by its cowardice."

Chapter Five

PEOPLE ON THE MOVE

As a public figure and an activist, DuBois was overmatched. Booker Washington enjoyed an eminence among whites and exerted an influence on the general life of Negroes that was unprecedented. His policy was to keep the post-Reconstruction pattern unbroken and to make the Negroes' lowly place in that pattern secure. It was not so much that he was against his own people, but that he was for civil peace. Himself a consummate politician "working on the inside", he was against Negroes participating in politics beyond the extent of going to "Southern white people. . . for advice concerning the casting of their ballots." He opposed any process of socialization for the Negro that seemed to challenge the white man's concept of the Negro. In short, Booker Washington accepted a subordinate place for Negroes in American life.

Nevertheless, a number of Negroes managed to lift themsleves above the masses, and even to exert some influence on Negro life. DuBois often referred to them as the "talented tenth". They were those who taught in the better Negro high schools, who preached from the pulpits of the more enlightened churches, and who edited the Negro newspapers that had national distribution—the Chicago *Defender,* the *Afro-American,* and the *Black Dispatch.* They wrote books, like DuBois' own *The Souls of Black Folk,* and Charles W. Chesnutt's *The House Behind the Cedars,* and Kelly Miller's *Race Adjustment.* They were the people who fought the local battles that resulted in the establishment of such hospitals as Provident in Chicago, Mercy in Philadelphia, Freedman's in Washington, and Homer Phillips in St. Louis.

Except in the case of DuBois, who even then had an international reputation as a scholar, and in the case of Dr. Daniel Hale Williams, who performed the first successful operation on the human heart, the accomplishments of these men and women were not widely known outside the race. But they were important. They were marks to shoot for. They sustained Negro morale. They were testimony to the fact that white men had no monopoly of intellect and purpose. By the wholesome exercise of their skills and the humane use of their learning, these Negro men and women helped to keep the American conscience alive.

And as ironic as it may seem, so did outbreaks of racial violence, particularly when they occurred in the North. As a matter of fact, explosions of anti-Negro feeling in the South —night-riding, mob-action and lynching—drew scant attention in the rest of the country; for the general attitude was that the race problem was the South's problem, and the South should be left free to handle it. But in the summer of 1908, a vicious eruption of race hatred in Springfield, Illinois, indicated how unjustified that attitude was. A white mob, spawned by lies and rumor, raged through the city for three days, killing Negroes, destroying their property, and forcing them to flee.

The NAACP and the Urban League

When the first shock of surprise and fear wore off, there were those in the North who took a second look at the race problem. "Who realizes the seriousness of the situation?" William English Walling, a distinguished New York journalist asked; "and what large and powerful body of citizens is ready. . . to aid?" Joined by philosopher John Dewey, eminent lawyers, Moorfield Storey and Oswald G. Villard, critic-novelist William D. Howells, and the pioneer social workers, Jane Addams and Mary Ovington, Walling issued a call "to believers in democracy to join a national conference for the discussing of present evils, the voicing of protests and the renewal of the struggle for civil and political liberty."

The group that responded to that call was not large, but most of its members had access to sources of power. Moreover, they held to the principle and followed the practice of interracial cooperation. In 1910, this group founded the National Association for the Advancement of Colored People, and in the following year the National Urban League was established.

In the pages of its official magazine, *The Crisis*, edited by DuBois, the NAACP began immediately to make its position known: it was for racial equality. Immediately, too, it carried the struggle for equality into the courts. With the help of Felix Frankfurter and Arthur Spingarn, who volunteered their services, the Association was successful in having the constitutionality of the Fifteenth Amendment reaffirmed; in invalidating the "Grandfather Clauses" that had frustrated Negro voting in the post-Reconstruction South; and in winning a decision against residential segregation. Though in their practical results, these proved to be somewhat hollow victories, the Association was not discouraged.

Meantime, it probed at the political front. DuBois' editorials cautioned Negroes to re-examine their loyalty to the Republican Party. "Let us not close our eyes. Let us look at the Democrats." They looked, and some saw a few they liked, including Woodrow Wilson, the Democrats' presidential nominee in 1912. Southern-born though he was, Wilson sounded good in the election campaign of that year. "I want to assure them [the colored people]", he pledged at one point, "that should I become President of the United States they may count upon me for absolute fair dealing, for everything by which I could assist in advancing the interests of their race. . . ."

Four years later, having served out one term, Wilson not only did not sound good, but, so far as Negroes were concerned, he had done much worse. He had refused to see their leaders, some of whom he had charged with "impudence", or to listen to their white friends. He had pooh-poohed proposals for anti-lynching legislation as unnecessary and "unwarranted". And by executive order, he had reversed federal usage and introduced segregation into every government department in Washington.

Just the same, in some respects the times were propitious for Negroes and for progress in race relations.

The Race Problem Moves North

Europe was at war. The recall of thousands of European nationals—Hungarians and Poles, Italians, Greeks, Austrians, and Czechs—had created a manpower shortage in the industries of the Midwest and the North. Meanwhile, the boll weevil and two successive years of flood in the planting season had ravaged the South's cotton, and Negroes, the great majority of agricultural workers, found less and less employment. They began to move. Encouraged by employment agents, Negroes began to move out of the South in such numbers as to make the exodus of the 1870's and '80's resemble a holiday excursion. The white South took alarm. Repression, intimidation, and renewed violence were the first reactions, but the exodus did not stop or slacken. Then the South tried reason and conciliation—often weakened by a tone of condescendence. The editor of a Texas newspaper wrote that "Negroes can do more for themselves and humanity by working the fields of the South. . . . the Negro who will work and who will keep his place can find more real happiness in the South than he will ever find in the cities of the North."

The Atlanta *Constitution,* the South's most influential newspaper, did better. "We must be fair to the Negro. There is no use beating about the bush. We have not shown that fairness in the past, nor are we showing it today, either in justice before the law, or facilities accorded for educations, or in other directions." Even the governor of Mississippi, the state most notorious for backwardness and anti-Negro feeling, adopted the tone of the *Constitution.* Governor Theodore Bilbo pleaded for "fair dealing" for the Negroes, "an end to abuses, and higher wages".

Still, Negroes poured out of the South in trainloads. A million of them left in less than two years.

But adjustments in the North were not easy, either for the ever-arriving blacks or the long-resident whites. A pattern of residential segregation by national origin and cultural heritage, as well as by race, already established in most northern cities, tended to fix rigidly for Negroes. Whereas before, a few Negroes, frustrated by lack of economic opportunity, had lived in the poorest sections of cities, now there were many. In Chicago, for instance, one Negro newspaper reported that Negroes "were packed in like sardines". And Chicago was typical. While Negroes paid exorbitant rents, the tax-supported services they received were minimal. School buildings were neglected and the best-qualified teachers were assigned elsewhere. Certain city-owned-and-operated hospitals became known as *Negro* hospitals, and medical service in them declined. Neighborhood merchants, most of whom were white and did not live among their customers, charged outrageous prices for inferior food and merchandise. Building codes, sanitary codes, and fire regulations that were enforced in other sections, were simply overlooked in those areas where Negroes lived. The Negroes' efforts to escape met with resistance, and when a few did succeed in moving into better neighborhoods, white residents quickly withdrew, and in the new place the cycle of crowding, neglect, and deterioration repeated itself, almost as if it were a phenomenon in the natural order of things.

But there were a few organizations and more than a few people who would not accept the vitiation of Negro urban life as natural and inevitable. After all, the American creed was not a mere pious fraud (though there were cynics who said it was), and the unfolding process of American socialization seemed to support the fact that it was not. Some gave no thought to the creed at any time, but many remembered it some of the time—in fits of crises and starts of alarm—and a few tried to act upon it most of the time.

Individuals like Julius Rosenwald and Jane Addams tried to improve the quality of Negro life in the Midwest; the Spingarn brothers tried in New York and along the eastern seaboard. In the South, W. W. Alexander, Robert Eleazer, and J. H. Dillard—the latter using the resources of the Anna T. Jeanes Fund—were working for the same end. The NAACP and the National Urban League, both chiefly supported by private philanthropy, broadened their activities. Opening branches in the larger cities, these organizations held conferences, conducted educational programs on urban life, and tried to open doors to new opportunities in employment and in the labor movement. Though nothing yielded easily—in government, politics, around the conference table, and in courts of law—Negroes and their white friends pressed and propagandized and pressed again. By the time the United States entered the war in April, 1917, there had been enough activity on the racial front to promote a sense of Negro morale higher than it had been since the end of Reconstruction.

World War

And it remained surprisingly high, in spite of incidents and expressed attitudes that seemed calculated to lower it.

Nearly fifty Negroes were lynched in 1917, and in July of that year, just four months after the United States made her declaration of war, forty more were killed by mobs in East St. Louis, Illinois. Draft boards in the South called up thirty-two percent of all Negroes who registered, as against twenty-six percent of whites. In service, Negroes complained of segregation in training camps, and of inferior facilities, such as YMCA and Red Cross canteens. There were frequent clashes between Negro soldiers and white soldiers and civilians. As a result of a clash in Houston, Texas, thirteen colored soldiers were sentenced to be hanged and fourteen were imprisoned for life.

The federal government was concerned with these "distempers", as one official described them. The War Information office revived an old slogan: United We Stand—Divided We Fall. President Wilson spoke out against lynching and anti-Negro violence—a thing he had not done publicly before. Several government departments in Washington began to re-examine and gradually to change their discriminatory practices. The Department of Labor set up a special division to deal with "Negro problems", and chose a Negro to head it. The War Department, which opened a camp for the training of Negro officers, appointed a Negro as a special assistant. Other Negroes were given comparable posts. They served with the War Committee on Public Information, the Army YMCA, the Red Cross, and the National Council for Defense. Eighteen were appointed directors in the War Food Administration. Robert R. Moton, who had succeeded Booker Washington as Principal of Tuskegee, was sent to France to bolster the morale of Negro troops.

There were 20,000 Negroes in the U. S. Army and the National Guard when America entered the war, and 375,000 more were drafted. Most served as laborers—stevedores, truck drivers, and depot scavengers in the army; messmen and orderlies in the navy. But there were Negro fighting units, too. The 369th Infantry lost more than a thousand men in battle, and had the Croix de Guerre pinned to its colors. The 370th Infantry, which was integrated with a French division, was fighting when the Armistice came. Sixty of its men won the Croix de Guerre, twenty-one were awarded the Distinguished Service Cross, and one was awarded the Distinguished Service Medal. John J. Pershing, Commanding General of the U. S. Army, described the 367th Infantry as "one of the best in the American Expeditionary Force". The first American soldiers to receive the highest decoration of the French government were Negroes. The first American soldiers to reach the Rhine were Negroes. Nearly the last Americans to die in combat were Negroes.

In the capacity of private citizens, Negroes did all that was asked of them and more than was generally expected. They, too, planted "victory gardens" and held Liberty Bond rallies, where they set high quotas and oversubscribed them time and again. In their churches, lodge rooms, and private homes, Negro women knitted sweaters, scarves, and caps for the army, and made bandages for the Red Cross. In war industries, Negro men worked at jobs that had previously been denied them. They were in the shipyards as riveters, the steel mills as puddlers and hearthmen, and in the munitions plants as machine operators. They worked on the railroads and in the merchant marines, in food processing plants, and in the automotive shops.

"Let us not hesitate," DuBois had admonished his people in the first months of the war. "Let us, while this war lasts, forget our special grievances and close ranks shoulder to shoulder with our white citizens and the allied nations that are fighting for democracy."

And the record shows that Negroes did just that.

PART III

THE CHALLENGE OF DEMOCRACY, 1918-1954

Chapter Six

"PEACE" AND THE "RETURN TO NORMALCY"

WHEN the war ended it seemed that the democracy Negroes had helped to save was not meant for them. The country was weary of war, and the slogans that had inspired it were soon forgotten. As the first postwar president, Warren G. Harding, put it, the thing was "to return to normalcy", to conservatism, to the *status quo ante,* as quickly as possible. Still a great many Americans saw that objective threatened everywhere—by the International Workers of the World and organized labor; by Progressivism under the Wisconsin politician, Robert M. LaFollette; by Eugene V. Debs' brand of Socialism, and by Bolshevism and Negro intransigence, considered the deadliest threats of all.

The Swing Toward the Right

If sporadic outburts of "radical" agitation seemed to suggest that the idea of social reconstruction was still alive, they also had the substantive effect of further inciting conservative reaction, and this was most dramatically symbolized in the resurrection of the Ku Klux Klan. An organization of robed and hooded men, the Klan projected a program "to unite native-born white Christians for concerted action in the preservation of American institutions and the supremacy of the white race". Although it was against Jews, Catholics, Asiatics, and foreign-born whites, its principal, most vulnerable and exposed target was Negroes. Whether or not all the twenty-five anti-Negro riots in the summer and fall of 1919, and the seventy-five lynchings in that same year could be laid at the door of the Klan, its boast of members in high

47

places in public life and the display of its masked minions North and South certainly contributed to the growth of anti-Negro feeling in the early post-war years.

Negroes, however, were no longer willing to yield to tactics of coercion. Something had wrought a change in the Negro people. Their war experiences had toughened them and given them a new conception of American life and of their place in it. The docility in the face of oppression that once was thought to characterize them had vanished. In the white press they were referred to as "new Negroes". They were determined to keep alive their dreams of what America could be. They were determined to defend themselves—and they did. In the riots of 1919, in Longview, Texas, in Washington, D. C., in Chester, Pennsylvania, in Omaha, Nebraska, and in Chicago, they defended themselves with such vigor as to alarm Congress, which called on the Justice Department to investigate. Many people in and out of government accepted the view of a Representative from South Carolina, who held that the "incendiary utterances" of Negroes were "responsible for racial antagonism". After an investigation that lasted three weeks, the Justice Department gave official support to this opinion, and then went on to deplore the Negroes' "ill-governed reaction toward race-rioting. . . the threat of retaliatory measures in connection with lynching. . . more openly expressed demands for social equality. . . [and] the identification of the Negro with such radical organizations as the I. W. W. and an outspoken advocacy of the Bolshevik doctrine."

This last charge was especially ridiculous. It is true that the Communist Party tried to win Negroes to its cause, and that its legal arm, the International Labor Defense, gave a few Negroes legal aid, but, excepting the policy of racial equality, Negroes repudiated Communist ideology. At no time in the years from 1919 to 1933 and beyond could the Party boast of as many as five hundred Negro members; and, indeed, the most reliable reports for the year 1928, when Communist proselytizing among Negroes was at its height, set the figure at two hundred. What is absurd about the other charges is the wording of them—the implication that it was morally and socially reprehensible for Negroes to defend themselves when they were put upon, and the implication that their demands for equality were subversive and anti-American. The truth of the matter is that the Negroes' demands were the measure of both their belief in democracy as an attainable goal and their new-found pride in themselves.

The "New Negro" and the Old Problems

The pride had obvious sources. For an instance, there was the race chauvinism promoted by a West Indian-born Negro named Marcus Garvey, who led a Back-to-Africa movement in the 1920's. Though American Negroes were not about to "go back to Africa", where few had ever been, Garvey gave them a fresh sense of themselves, a new awareness of their history, and a hearty pride in their African ancestry. His organization, the Universal Negro Improvement Association, claimed 4,000,000 members in 1922. "Up, you mighty race! Back to Africa!" Garvey exhorted. "Ancient conquerors, statesmen and artists came out of Africa," he said, claiming Hannibal, the first Bernadotte of Sweden, Pushkin the Russian poet, Beethoven, and Alexander Dumas; "and they were *your* people. . . . Let Africa be a bright star among the constellations of nations."

Up, you mighty race was the theme of all the exhorters —and in the postwar years there were many, white as well as black. They were a various company, from mystics who were called "god" and "divine", to charlatans, to the recognized leaders of traditional organizations, but each in his own way kindled race pride, gave off currents of impatience, and incited the "ill-governed reaction" that expressed

itself in so many ways. Older organizations, such as the
NAACP, the National Urban League, and the Association
for the Study of Negro Life and History doubled their efforts in court, Congress, and conference, to win for Negroes
a more equitable share of democratic rights and privileges.
New organizations, such as the American Negro Labor Congress and the bi-racial Commission on Interracial Cooperation, came into being and took off in other directions. The
Friends of Negro Freedom, another bi-racial group, func-
tioned to protect Negro tenants in urban areas. The Colored
Housewives League, founded in 1926, mounted a campaign
to discourage Negroes from buying where they could not
work. Both as individuals and as members of groups, prominent white people joined the crusade for Negro rights.
Clarence Darrow and Arthur Garfield Hays, two of the most
celebrated lawyers in the country, took up the legal defense
of a Detroit Negro who, in repulsing a mob attack on his
home in a white neighborhood, killed a white man. In
Atlanta, Georgia, a group of white women formed the Association of Southern Women for the Prevention of Lynching. The Atlanta *Constitution,* the South's outstanding
newspaper, commented favorably on this "unprecedented"
development, and went on to urge Congress to pass an anti-
lynching bill.

There was, too, a gradual feedback from the continuing
civic disturbances to local governments and to sociological
scholarship. Following the example set by Chicago after the
bloody riot of 1919, municipal authorities in some cities
created *ad hoc* racial commissions or committees to deal
with the problems of bi-racial living. Washington, Philadelphia, New York, and Boston had such councils, whose
duty it was "to quench, if possible, the fires of racial antagonism". Meanwhile, scholars of both races tried to get
at the roots of the problem. All sorts of research, both
commissioned and independent, was undertaken. Howard

Odum and Guy B. Johnson, at the University of North Carolina, studied patterns of social interaction—and Odum used his findings as material for two novels. Robert Park and Franklin Frazier, at the University of Chicago, examined the Negro family. At Fisk University, Charles S. Johnson, and at Northwestern, Melville T. Herskovits investigated Negro acculturation. Books, monographs, and essays poured out in a steady stream, and long before academic activity reached a climax in the publication of Gunnar Myrdal's *An American Dilemma* in 1943, no aspect of the American race problem had been left unexplored. But almost none of the new knowledge was put to work at solving basic problems in race relations. Most of it went into masters' theses and doctoral dissertations. Research material—some of it soon to be outdated by changing conditions—gathered dust on out-of-the-way shelves. Racial commissions became mere honorary bodies, without programs or power.

Creative Expression

If the Negro's new sense of race and of self was a "spiritual emancipation", as Alain Locke, a Negro professor of philosophy, said, it was nowhere more evident than in his rejection of the old stereotypes, in his refusal to conform to whatever was anciently expected of him, in his repudiation of social and cultural mimicry, and in his determination to reveal himself truly in all his misunderstood and misprized variety. The revelations came in a storm of creative activity in literature and the theatre, in music and the dance.

Broadway, the arbiter of popular cultural tastes, which was just then beginning its permanent love affair with the Negro music called jazz, welcomed such Negro "vocalists" as Ethel Waters, and Bessie and Mamie Smith singing the blues, and the jazz songs of Duke Ellington and Jimmie Lunceford. It applauded dancers like "Bojangles" Robinson and Josephine Baker, gyrating through the strenuous intricacies of dances called the Charleston, the Black Bottom, and the Lindy Hop. And Negro writers—poets and novelists —enjoying creative freedom for the first time, were no less uninhibited than the singers and dancers, and no less defiant of the socio-cultural tradition that hitherto required them to cater to the known expectations of white folks. If white people were pleased with what they saw, heard, and read, well and good. If they were not, it didn't matter. "We are no longer concerned with telling white people what they want to hear," declared Langston Hughes, one of the first "New Negro" writers, in 1928. He was speaking for most of them, including Claude McKay, who wrote:

If we must die, let it not be like hogs,
While round us bark the mad and hungry dogs,
Making their mock at our accursed lot . . . .

He was also speaking for Countee Cullen, who wrote:

She even thinks that up in heaven
Her class lies late and snores,
While poor black cherubs rise at seven
To do celestial chores.

And for Rudolph Fisher and Wallace Thurman, whose novels revealed what life was like in the Negro ghetto; and for Jessie Fauset, whose first novel of Negro middle class life was rejected by one publisher who reminded Miss Fauset that "white readers don't expect Negroes to be like this". White readers did not expect Negroes to be like the characters in Jean Toomers' *Cane* either, or like those in Walter White's *Fire in the Flint,* or like those in Hughes' own *Not Without Laughter* and *The Ways of White Folks.*

All these, and more, violently shook the old notions of what Negroes were and what Negro life was like. All these, and more, including the sudden French-inspired interest in Negro (African) art, and the winning of the Goncourt Prize by Réné Maran with his Negro novel *Batuola*—all these

suggested to serious white writers and artists what the pos-
sibilities were for the creative uses of Negro life and the
American race situation. Thus, Eugene O'Neill, often con-
sidered the greatest American dramatist, was moved to write
"The Emperor Jones" and "All God's Chillun Got Wings".
Paul Green won a Pulitzer Prize with his play of Southern
Negro life, "In Abraham's Bosom". George Gershwin, who
was later to base his opera "Porgy and Bess" on a novel
of Negro life, wrote the concerto "Rhapsody in Blue", em-
ploying the melodic themes of jazz. Julia Peterkin's novel
Scarlet Sister Mary, Carl Van Vechten's *Nigger Heaven,*
Sherwood Anderson's *Dark Laughter,* and DuBose Heyward's *Mamba's Daughters* all appeared, were praised
(sometimes extravagantly), and widely read within the span
of the decade from 1922 to 1932. Never before had interest
in the Negro and his life been so high. Never since has the
interest found expression in so great a variety of ways.

But an end to all this was in sight. The entrepreneurs
awoke to the fact of this interest, and commercialism took
over. Having no publishing houses, no music companies, no
art galleries, or concert halls, Negroes could give only moral
support and encouragement to the artists and writers who
were trying to tell as much of the painful truth as they
knew. Negroes could not prevent the take-over by the imita-
tors and the magazine and newspaper feature writers, who
changed the emphasis and the direction of the "Negro Renaissance". Terms like "exotic", "colorful", "primitive", and
"pagan" came to be attached to it, and to Negro life in
big city ghettoes as well. Sight-seeing busloads of whites
were regularly and routinely scheduled to tour New York's
Harlem, Chicago's South Side, and New Orleans' Basin and
Rampart Streets. The exotic and primitive were played up
in "Negro" night clubs (where Negroes were not admitted),
and in cheap novels with titles like *Sweet Man, The Blacker
the Berry,* and *Prancing Nigger.* The genuine passion, the

subtly ironic and satiric commentary of jazz were diluted by white musicians who did not have the emotional experience to sustain them. The blues became "torch songs" when sung by white entertainers, who had never known the heartbreak and outrage of being black.

But an end to all this commercial exploitation of Negro life, too, was in sight. And when it came, it put an end to many other things besides—the postwar era of prosperity, "normalcy", laissez-faire, and, most of all, it put an end to those attitudes expressed in such phrases as "rugged individualism", "free enterprise", and "the American way of life".

Chapter Seven

DEPRESSION, NEW DEAL, AND WORLD WAR II

ALTHOUGH the revolution that was heralded by the stock market collapse of 1929 was basically socio-economic, it had political consequences. This was especially true for Negroes, who had begun to loosen their sentimental ties to the Republican Party in 1924, when both the Democrats and the Progressives wooed them with forthright declarations against distinctions based on color and with promises of fair representation in political councils. In 1928, the ties were further loosened when it became clear that the Republicans, having by-passed Negro leaders in the Party, meant to pursue a lily-white line. Herbert Hoover, the Party's presidential candidate, carried Virginia, North Carolina, Tennessee, Kentucky, Florida, and Texas, partly because his opponent, Alfred E. Smith, was a Catholic, and partly because Hoover was eloquently and completely silent on the "Negro question". Victory in these Southern states could mean only one thing—the Republican party no longer professed a special concern for Negroes.

Moreover, while the Republicans were soliciting white votes in the South, the Democrats made it quite clear that they wanted Negro support in the North, and they went to lengths never taken by the Republicans to get it. Prominent Democrats joined Negroes in opposing the confirmation of John J. Parker, a reactionary North Carolinian, to the U.S. Supreme Court. In New York, the Democrats gave new meaning and influence to the United Colored Democracy when they made that segregated auxilary's leader, Ferdinand Q. Morton, one of the bosses of party patronage

55

in the state. In Illinois, the Democratic machine ran a Negro for national office in 1934, and Arthur W. Mitchell became the first black Democrat ever to sit in Congress. Besides, Negro Democrats—twelve altogether—were elected to state legislatures in Maryland, West Virginia, Pennsylvania, New York, and Illinois. The switch from the Republican to the Democratic party was quite evident in 1936, for President Franklin D. Roosevelt had proved himself sympathetic to Negro problems, and, by 1939, the Negroes' break with the Republican Party, which the *New York Times* called a "splendid revolt", was practically complete. Within a period of three or four years, the Negro people in the North had achieved political respectability and more political power than they had ever known.

Programs and Prospects

This new fact of American life was soon evident in the policies of President Roosevelt's "New Deal". Under this dispensation, the government took on a new and more extensive responsibility for the economic welfare of the people. The Roosevelt administration set up all sorts of agencies to carry out programs of recovery and relief. Though the National Industrial Recovery Act, which was designed to do exactly what the title suggests, touched Negroes only a little—since by and large Negroes were not in industry—other measures affected them a great deal. The Farm Security Administration (FSA), the Home Owners Loan Corporation, the National Youth Administration (NYA), and the Civilian Conservation Corps were created to benefit all the needy; and in order that Negroes might receive their share of the benefits, the President appointed race relations experts to these agencies. Though some of these appointees, such as W. W. Alexander of the FSA, and Aubrey Williams of the NYA were white, a considerable number were Negroes. Men like Ralph Bunche, Robert Weaver, and William Hastie served so effectively that doors slowly began to open to them and to other Negroes in the Departments of Commerce, Interior, Justice, and State.

Under the New Deal, 200,000 Negro youths were employed in conservation and reclamation projects during the worst years of the depression. The NYA enabled other thousands—young women as well as young men—to continue their education. Some 50,000 Negro farmers were granted government loans, and the average income of Negro farm families nearly doubled in three years. The Wages and Hours Bill boosted the wages of more than a million Negro non-farm workers, and although housing remained substandard, and even wretched, for the great majority of Negroes, government-sponsored construction of low-cost housing helped to relieve living conditions among low-income Negroes, as well as white people, in urban communities all over the country. Finally, the Works Progress Administration employed Negroes on many of its projects, gave relief in food and clothing to the unemployable, and aided Negro hospitals, colleges, community centers, and day nurseries in the South on the same basis that it aided such institutions for whites.

If these federal activities had little effect on racial segregation *per se*, they must have had some salutary influence on race relations and group interaction. At least they did not encourage discrimination; rather, they chipped and weakened it, if only ever so little. The federal courts, too, began chipping away at discrimination and segregation, particularly in public education. In 1938, when, rather than admit a Negro to the white public university, the state of Missouri offered to pay the cost of his legal training in an institution outside the state, the U. S. Supreme Court ruled that failure to provide equal education within the state violated the U. S. Constitution. Two years later, Negroes were being admitted on the graduate level to "white" universities in four

Southern states. Thus the enlargement of freedom and opportunities for Negroes progressed bit by bit. Less publicized,
but also indicative of a gradual change, was the fact that a
few private white schools and colleges actively encouraged
Negro students with offers of scholarships; and three universities—Harvard, Chicago, and New York—each appointed a
Negro to faculty rank.

When the powerful labor leader, John L. Lewis, withdrew
the United Mine Workers from the American Federation of
Labor and began organizing workers on an industry-wide
basis, he made it clear that considerations of race and color
should not affect membership in the new Congress of Industrial Organizations (CIO). Some of the most influential
affiliates of the CIO, including the Packinghouse Workers,
the United Auto Workers, the Mine Workers, and the Steel
Workers, had large and active Negro memberships, from
which qualified Negroes were elected to national offices in
the unions and to governing boards of the international
CIO.

The Continuing Challenge

But the pace of these changes, which affected a relative
few, seemed slow, and the benefits limited, and the mass of
Negroes remained impatient and restive. Like people everywhere, the more they won, the more conscious they were of
what remained to be won. Their newspapers and magazines
kept up a steady barrage of propaganda and exhortation;
their organizations kept up a steady pressure of activities and
protest. In the mid-1930's the National Urban League
staged a "Jobs-for-Negroes" campaign, which, while it
resulted in the employment of some Negroes in national
chain stores in cities as distant as Atlanta, Georgia and
Chicago, Illinois, had an altogether different consequence in
New York. When the white merchants in Harlem refused
their "reasonable demands", frustrated Negroes, further em-

bittered by rumors of police brutality, rioted, smashing into stores and doing thousands of dollars of damage, and making off with millions of dollars worth of goods.

The Harlem riot was exceptional. Negro leaders usually were able to control and direct action constructively within the Negro community, which in many ways was a separate world. It was materially impoverished, it was backward and underdeveloped, it was even alienated, but it was not alien to the white world. The same cultural totems and social symbols that prevailed in one, prevailed and had authority in the other. Negroes had their churches and their schools, too, their libraries and newspapers. Their hotels and restaurants, their theatres and clubs, and all their social and cultural institutions were as American as baseball. While protesting its forced existence, Negro leaders tried to make the best of their separate world. They also tried to make it a source of pride, even while they deplored the proscriptive prejudice that set it apart from the American world at large.

So there has been a certain ambivalence. "Negro History Week", which is observed annually in the colored community, promotes the race's self-esteem, but also points up the fact that white historians underplay the part that Negroes have had in the development of America. Negro newspapers serve an important function, but Negroes count it a credit to have stories of their accomplishments appear in the white press. When a prominent Negro, such as a Lena Horne or a Sammy Davis, Jr., marries into the white race, Negroes are torn between a feeling of being let down and a feeling of pride that one of them has been accepted in the white world.

Advances and Advantages

Although this emotional ambivalence is perhaps not the least of the consequences of the problems in the colored community, Negro leaders have given it only pe-

ripheral attention. Instead, they have addressed themselves
to upgrading Negro education, to securing better housing, to
broadening employment opportunities, and to attaining
effective political power locally and nationally. All Negro
leaders and their organizations have not approached these
problems from the same point of view, or sought to solve
them in the same ways. The NAACP has not always seen
eye to eye with the National Urban League, nor the Congress of Racial Equality with the Southern Youth Congress.
There have been divisions and discord within the Negro
world. There has been leadership rivalry. Nevertheless, when
it has come to interaction between the Negro and the white
world, Negro leaders have generally put their differences
aside, and the Negro people have rallied behind a united
leadership.

An impressive instance of this occurred when Hitler
plunged Europe into war and American became the "arsenal
of Democracy". Throughout 1940, as increasing numbers of
workers were needed to keep the war plants humming, the
employment situation of Negroes did not change appreciably. "Negro jobs", of which there were fewer than formerly,
were the least desirable, lowest paid. Though the federal
government laid down the rule that the Defense Training
Program was to accept trainees on a non-discriminatory
basis, and even though the Office of Production Manage-
ment set up a special branch for Negro training and employment, the opportunity to acquire skills that might lead
to better jobs remained closed. Negro leaders knew from
experience that it was not enough for the government
to oppose discrimination in principle: government must act
against it.

In January of 1941, the chief officers of the NAACP, the
National Urban League, and the Brotherhood of Sleeping
Car Porters drew up their grievances and demands and pre-
sented them to Washington. If nothing was done to meet

their demands, they said, they would organize one hundred thousand Negroes to march on the nation's Capital. Government officials and Mrs. Eleanor Roosevelt, the wife of the President, met with the Negro leaders, and attempted to dissuade them, but nothing came of it.

Finally President Roosevelt issued Executive Order 8802. It declared that "there shall be no discrimination in the employment of workers in defense industries and in Government because of race, creed, color, or national origin." It established a Committee on Fair Employment Practices to investigate complaints and seek to correct violations. The doors to training and employment gradually opened to Negroes. One hundred thousand went into aircraft factories in skilled and semi-skilled occupations. More than three hundred thousand went into other industries where, as they responded to training and production demands increased, many of them were upgraded.

The cohesiveness of the Negro people was influential in other ways, too. It certainly helped to arouse the conscience of the country, and to awaken the realization that the things for which the war was being fought could not be won by blood alone. When Negroes protested discrimination in the armed services, the government took steps to reduce it. Negroes were put on draft boards in more than a thousand towns and cities. One Negro was appointed an executive assistant to the Chief of Selective Service. Hitherto restricted to work as stewards (waiters, valets, kitchen help) in the Navy, that branch of the service began accepting Negroes in general ratings, and by 1945, Negroes were not only receiving training as naval officers, but the Navy was making other gestures in the direction of the desegregation. Hitherto, no Negro had served in the Marine Corps in any capacity, but by 1944, there were 17,000 Negro Marines, and a handful of these were officers. The Air Force began recruiting Negroes and training them as fighter and bomber pilots in 1940, but, as with the Army, desegregation in this the most "glamorous" service was not fully accomplished until the Korean conflict. Nearly a million Negro men and women served in the armed forces in World War II. They were posted in all the theatres of war, and in all the military establishments at home and abroad.

As civilians, Negroes worked in the Merchant Marine, and four of them commanded mixed crews on Liberty (cargo) ships. Negroes worked in the Office of Civilian Defense, the Office of Price Administration, the Office of War Information, the War Production Board, the Manpower Commission, and the United Service Organization. Most were in minor clerical capacities, but some were highly-trained economists, psychologists, lawyers, and journalists, and they worked in their specialties. When the *ad hoc* agencies began to dissolve after the war, a good many Negroes transferred to permanent departments of government, where there was no official bar to advancement to the highest civil service classification.

New Perspectives and New Power

But for all these new advantages and advances, and the beneficent influence of the federal government, problems remained. Some, indeed, had been aggravated. The war had not only freshened the tide of Negro migration from the non-industrial areas of the South, but had set running a tide of white migration as well. Beginning in 1941 and continuing through the war, nearly a thousand people a day, white and Negro, and mostly Southern, streamed into Los Angeles. San Francisco, Portland, Oregon, and Seattle, Washington, were flooded, too. Though jobs were plentiful, housing, school, and recreation facilities were not, and competition was fierce. Civic machinery was not geared to operate in this new situation. Ghettoes grew denser. Social instability increased. Crimes rates spurted upward, and tension stayed unusually high. The city of Portland was constantly at flash point. In 1942, a riot pitted whites against Negroes and Mexican-Americans in Los Angeles. When the city authorities of Detroit and the governor of Michigan were unable to quell a riot in 1943, the President of the U. S. sent 5,000 soldiers to restore order and keep the peace.

Such forthright action by President Roosevelt and his successor, Harry S Truman, and the continuing work of private interracial groups encouraged those who believed that the recently proclaimed "four freedoms" were meant for everyone. Moreover, the Negroes' growing political strength in the North, their greater economic security, and their determination were not lost on politicians and elected public officials. When the war ended, there was already a campaign afoot to create a permanent and more powerful Fair Employment Practices Commission. Before the war ended, liberal white Southerners joined with prominent Negroes to urge a "new morality. . . consistent with the principles for which we as a nation" fought throughout the world.

The "new morality" was not exclusively American by any means. It was a universal concept, and it was, hopefully, to be embodied in the United Nations Organization.

The representatives of the fifty-one nations that met in San Francisco in the early summer of 1945 were very much aware of the dark-skinned members among them—Liberians, Ethiopians, Haitians, Indians, and the several American Negroes who had been accredited by the U. S. Department of State. Every delegate realized that lasting universal peace, which was the object, could rest only on the principle and practice of human rights and human equality. The first U.N. document did not blink the fact. "We the people [of the U.N.] . . . reaffirm faith in fundamental human rights, in the dignity and worth of the human person . . . and respect for, and observance of, human rights and fundamental freedoms of all without distinction as to race, sex, language or religion . . ."

Believing in the sincerity of this, Negroes subscribed to the NAACP's "Appeal to the World, A Statement on the Denial of Human Rights to Minorities in the Case of Citizens of Negro Descent in the United States and an Appeal to the United Nations for Redress." But when this was presented to the U.N., the U.S. Attorney General was dismayed "that any citizens of this country should feel compelled to go over the heads of their government in seeking redress of grievances".

The Attorney General's exception to the NAACP's appeal was not entirely unreasonable. Though slow, progress within the national framework was steady and obvious, and this progress continued through the 1940's and early 1950's. The compulsive logic of the Negroes' thrust forward could not be laughed off. When President Truman's Committee on Civil Rights recommended the elimination of segregation from every aspect of American life and the enactment of a Fair Employment Practices Act to prohibit discrimination in private employment, only a tight corps of die-hard racists in the South raised more than token protest. Both Presidents Truman and Eisenhower appointed Negroes to high places—a Governor of the Virgin Islands, an Assistant Secretary of Labor, a federal judge, and a member of the Federal Trade Commission. Only a few months after taking office in 1953, President Eisenhower quietly brought about desegregation of places of public accommodation in the nation's capital.

Meantime, the federal courts had been taking a closer look at restrictive laws and practices. The U. S. Supreme Court, especially, had been moving toward a more liberal interpretation of the Constitution. In 1943, it ruled that the exclusion of Negroes from jury rolls was unconstitutional. In 1946, it held that state laws requiring segregation on public carriers could not apply in interstate transportation. Two years later, the Court decreed that private covenants which barred Negroes from owning and occupying real estate were without legal force. And, in 1950, the Court declared that the inferiority of a publicly-supported Negro educational institution was an intolerable discrimination, and that Negroes must be granted educational equality with whites.

The ruling in this case, which was specific to the public University of Texas, did not effect the doctrine of "separate but equal", which had prevailed in the South and Border states for more than half a century. Actually, though the "separate" had been rigidly applied, the "equal" never was, and separate Negro schools, libraries, and accommodations and services in publicly supported facilities of all kinds were woefully inferior to those provided for whites. Negroes had pointed this out all along, and as far back as 1945, the NAACP had determined to challenge the doctrine of "separate but equal" with a legal test of the idea that racial segregation itself is abhorrent to the principles of democracy. The testing began in 1950, when a suit to admit (Negro) children to public schools without regard to race was filed in a federal court in South Carolina. For four years, and in four separate suits, the testing continued, and was finally brought to the highest court in the land. Then, in 1964, the Supreme Court outlawed school segregation by ruling that separate schools were "inherently unequal" and that they violated the Fourteenth Amendment to the Constitution, which guarantees all citizens equal protection of the laws.

PART IV

"THE UNIVERSAL DECLARATION OF HUMAN RIGHTS," 1954-1967

Chapter Eight

THE NEW NEGRO
SELF-IMAGE

THE 1954 edict of the Court was followed the next year
by an injunction to the states to "proceed with all deliber-
ate speed". These measures were met with angry opposition
in all the Southern states. While the Border states moved
slowly to obey the law, Southern states resisted by "all
legal means". The new law aroused old arguments and older
fears, not the least of which was the argument of the "hal-
lowed Southern way of life", and the fears of "social equality"
and "intermarriage". The Southern states, like Georgia, Alabama, Mississippi, and Louisiana, where the racist White
Citizens Council used economic reprisals against Negroes,
and where the Ku Klux Klan and other extremists groups
used terror and violence, Negroes were too intimidated to
attempt to exercise their rights. Virginia authorities initiated
"massive resistance" and erected "legal" barriers against
compliance with the law. They closed some schools rather
than integrate them. They legalized the expenditure of public monies for tuition grants to students who did not care to
"mix", and hastily certified the hastily-organized white private schools where many of these students enrolled.

If this was brazen defiance, the Governor of Arkansas
outdid it. Claiming the right to interpose the authority of
the State between the law of the land and the federal power
to enforce it, Governor Faubus called on the state militia
to prevent nine Negro children from entering an all-white
public high school in Little Rock. Sworn to uphold the law
and to protect the rights of all citizens, black and white,

President Eisenhower ordered federal troops into the city. But he had no authority over the state's education system, and he could do nothing when the Governor ordered all the high schools in the city closed. The ugly story made headlines all over the world, and the schools remained closed for a year. But when they reopened in 1957, it was on a desegregated basis.

Resistance to the Court order took other forms in other places. Local and state authorites created ways to harry those who urged compliance with the law. Negro organizations bore the brunt of this harassment. The NAACP and the Legal Defense Fund were called subversive and "communist fronts". Negro public school teachers were threatened with the loss of their jobs for holding membership in these "subversive" groups. Negroes who expressed intent to enroll their children in formerly white schools, lost their jobs and their credit in stores and banks. Their mortgages were suddenly foreclosed, their insurance canceled, and often the convenience of buying food and fuel, even for cash, was denied them. Outright violence was another thing. Negro schools and churches, homes and places of business were bombed and set afire. Negro leaders were beaten. Murder was not uncommon.

Though its perpetrators were slow to realize it, violence was a questionable weapon in the cause of resistance to civil rights. It tended to generate sympathy for its victims. It repelled many people who ordinarily would have supported the *status quo ante* in civil rights. Thus even in the most backward states, where moderation on racial issues has never been counted a virtue and where violence is no sin, a few brave people spoke up for observance of the law. They were not necessarily for the doing away with segregation and the extension of Negro rights—though obviously some had been converted—but they were against the extremism of the Ku Klux Klan, and people of the type of

Eugene (Bull) Connor, the former Police Commissioner of Birmingham, Alabama, and Leander H. Perez, political boss of Plaquemine, Louisiana.

Other factors that helped, at least a little, to modify the South's first determination to resist at all cost were the underlying American assumption that the rule of law is preferable to the rule of men; the respect that Americans pay, however grudgingly at times, to "outside" opinions; and the deference they accord the moral authority of their country's Chief Executive, which, in this matter of civil rights, was exerted in support of judicial decree. Finally, the attitude, the strategy, and the behavior of the Negroes themselves—and of the not inconsiderable number of whites who were their friends and allies—were factors in bringing the posture of the South into nearer conformity to the posture of the nation as a whole, which, in 1955-56, could best be described as a posture of compromise.

New Tactics

Although Negroes did not abandon the old techniques of petition, political maneuver, court suits, and boycott, they initiated, in 1955, a tactic that was new to them. It was called non-violent resistance. Dr. Martin Luther King, Jr., who inspired the Negroes to use the tactic, described it: "We will take direct action against injustice without waiting for other agencies to act. We will not obey unjust laws or submit to unjust practices," he wrote. "We will do this peacefully, openly, cheerfully—because our aim is to persuade. We adopt the means of non-violence because our aim is a community at peace with itself. We will try to persuade with our words—but if our words fail we will try to persuade with our acts. We will always be willing to talk and seek fair compromise, but we are ready to suffer when necessary and even risk our lives to become witnesses to the truth as we see it."

The new tactic was surprisingly successful. Applied as a bus boycott in Montgomery, Alabama, it forced the issue of segregation in local public transportation into the courts, and when the Supreme Court ruled that segregation on Montgomery's buses was unconstitutional, dozens of Southern cities abandoned the practice of seating white passengers in front and Negroes in the rear of buses.

When four Negro college students, having been denied service at a "white" lunch counter, refused to leave, they opened a phase of the non-violent resistance campaign that swept the country and enlisted the aid of students and others, Negro and white. Local, state, and even a national organization—the Student Non-Violent Coordinating Committee—were formed to further the campaign. Students in "white" colleges as different in their general orientation as Vanderbilt University in Tennessee and Antioch College in Ohio, "sat in" in barbershops and lunch counters and picketed theatres that Negroes might be served. Old organizations such as the NAACP, the Urban League, and the Congress of Racial Equality lent their resources to this new phase of the struggle for liberalism and identity. The demonstrators turned to churches, parks, restaurants, and hotels. "Freedom rides" carried bi-racial groups from the North to challenge the South's non-compliance with the long-standing law against segregation in interstate travel and the facilities that were adjunct to it. Selective buying, too, was brought into play. Negroes refused to patronize stores where segregation was practiced and where employment policies discriminated against them. The resultant loss of revenue compelled many an individual merchant and several national merchandising chains to submit to the Negroes' demands for equality of treatment.

Not every place of business required this kind of pressure, nor did every community, even in the South, care to invite disorganization and the unfavorable image that sit-ins, boycotts, and protest picketing encouraged. In such communities, there was a laudable degree of voluntary compliance. But there were many more cities where segregation extremists controlled opinion, as they did in Albany, Georgia, Bogalusa, Louisiana, and Natchez, Mississippi. In these places, voluntary compliance was non-existent, and no amount of pressure worked. Even after the enactment of the sweeping Civil Rights Bill of 1964, segregation continued to prevail. Some places formerly open to the public evaded the law by declaring themselves private. A few restaurants and hotels in Georgia, Alabama, Florida, and Mississippi shut down altogether.

In 1965, following the enactment of a new voting rights bill, which outlawed racially discriminating limitations, Negroes were encouraged in their efforts to vote, and hundreds did register. But in hard-core segregationist towns and counties in the South, white registrars slowed down the process, or refused Negroes the necessary blanks, posted impossible hours for registration, or closed their offices.

Tokenism was the general rule in the upper South and Border states. Here, where the tide of opinion refused to set strongly either for or against segregation, the tactic of admitting one or two Negro pupils to previously all-white schools paid a token of respect to the law, while elaborate pseudo-legal barriers against the admisson of more defied the law's intent. Business and commercial concerns, desirous of keeping the patronage of whites without alienating the good will of Negroes, were cautious. The usual thing was to employ a Negro clerk, stenographer, or sales person, and make that Negro as inconspicuously visible as possible in a work force of twenty-five, fifty, or one hundred whites. But it is also true that some establishments, yielding to Negro protest and the admonishments and example of the federal government, had trouble finding Negroes who had even the modest qualifications of clerks and stenographers. And industries that had government contracts that committed them to non-discriminatory employment policies, often sought in vain for Negro machinists, draftsmen, engineers, and chemists. An appreciable number of highly trained and skilled Negroes were not to be found.

The Negro Revolution

And they were not to be found for reasons which Americans were only just beginning to recognize. Until the second World War and, subsequently, the modest successes of the Negro revolution in the 1950's, few Negroes dreamt of having careers in skilled occupations, and those who did dream had little opportunity to acquire training and skill. Craft unions generally barred Negroes from apprenticeships, and state license boards discriminated against them. Until the mid-1940's not a single Negro was licensed as a master plumber, and there were not a hundred Negroes certified as engineers in the whole country. No Negro college was accredited to train civil, mechanical, or electrical engineers until the 1950's, and Howard University and Meharry Medical College were the only Negro institutions where one could study medicine and dentistry. Negro certified public accountants could be ticked off on the fingers of one hand.

Other than Negroes, few people had considered these facts, and fewer still had felt the impact of them. But now again, as in the 1920's, there was a rush of interest. And this time it was more than temporary, and there was in it more than a modicum of good will, and more than a modicum, too, of enlightened self-interest. The political climate began to change as politicians came to realize that their careers were threatened by too adamant a stand against civil rights. In 1956, nineteen Southern senators and eighty-one congressmen had signed a "Southern Manifesto" subscribing to resistance to school integration, but the next year some of these legislators voted for a bill to assure equality of voting rights and to establish a federal Commission on Civil Rights. Even more of them changed their tune in 1960, when Negroes made a show of political strength by sending five members of their race to Congress, and by providing the margin of votes that gave John F. Kennedy a narrow victory over Richard Nixon. In 1964, Barry Goldwater, the Republican nominee, who as senator had voted against civil rights legislation, lost a chance for success when he refused to change his stand, and when he gave his campaign in the South a lily-white-party thrust. Even many Republicans refused to support him. A commitment to civil rights was becoming a prerequisite to winning elections almost everywhere but in the deep South.

And, as John F. Kennedy, the Democratic nominee, knew, the politics of the world situation required a national commitment to civil rights if America's leadership was to prevail. The United States could not hope to win the new brown and black nations to her side of the political and ideological struggle if she tolerated racism at home. The new color-conscious nations, having but recently overthrown white colonial domination, were suspicious. They made it known, in U. N. sessions and elsewhere, that the Negroes' position as a second-class citizen in the United States was a grave liability to any meaningful cooperation with America on the international front.

When this attitude was expressed by African nations, American Negroes reacted to it with enthusiastic affirmation. Indeed, some extremists among them over-reacted. The Black Muslims, who had adopted a degenerate form of the Islamic religion, denounced American democracy as a "delusion" and Christianity as a "fraud". The exhortation to Negroes to "go back to Africa" was heard once again, as it had been in the days of Marcus Garvey. Blaming all the world's troubles on American "imperialism" and the white man's "inborn perfidy", and pretending to see this nation's connivance in the murder of Patrice Lumumba, the first premier of independent Congo, a rabble of these extremists staged a riot in the U.N. that interrupted Ambassador Adlai Stevenson's first speech to the General Assembly.

The vast majority of Negroes were nowhere near as intemperate and unrealistic. They were, first of all, Americans. What the status of the new African states meant to them was an accession of their own dignity, an addition to their pride as black people, a new source of spiritual strength. What it meant was that they now had international allies. The Negro's image of himself, which patently had been changing since World War II, and which in any case was never the image white Americans had of him, began to emerge in bolder outline, with stronger lineaments. It was an image which the sit-ins, the freedom rides, and the protest marches had immeasurably sharpened, and America was at last becoming aware of it.

The American press, and, indeed, all the media of mass communication, reacted to this image responsibly. Newspapers generally accorded Negroes the conventional titles of courtesy, refrained from printing only crime stories about them, or only stories which ridiculed them. Motion picture producers began turning out films, such as "Home of the Brave", "Intruder in the Dust", and "Lost Boundaries", in which Negroes played roles that did not stereotye them as rascals and clowns. Broadway staged plays that dramatized heretofore unsuspected features of Negro middle class life. "Deep Are the Roots" explored the problems of a Negro ex-army officer, who, having achieved self-respect and initiative, is expected to jettison these attributes in order to survive as a civilian functioning in a predominently white social order. Television producers of popular entertainment were somewhat later in coming to treat Negro subject matter and Negro characters in other than a demeaning comic vein; but in the 1950's two of the three national television companies, whose programs are seen throughout the U. S., made honest and sympathetic documentaries of Negro life. From time to time, all three of the companies have featured Negro dramatic stars, concert singers, and entertainers of the calibre of Diana Sands and Frederick O'Neal, Leontyne Price and Marian Anderson, Lena Horne and Ella Fitzgerald, Duke Ellington, Louis Armstrong, and Harry Belafonte.

Negroes had long been prominent as athletes. Their history as representatives of the U. S. at the Olympic Games goes back to the 1920's. In the 1930's, Jesse Owens, the sprinter, was a super-star. Joe Louis became heavyweight boxing champion of the world in 1937, and held the title for twelve years. Sugar Ray Robinson, who did not retire from the boxing ring until 1965, was both lightweight and middleweight champion in the '40's and '50's.

In 1947, when the first Negro player broke into major league baseball, a part of the American public reacted antagonistically. It took Jackie Robinson's presence on the field with his white teammates as a threat to the "color line". The dissenters were numerous enough and vocal enough to bring pressure on some major league owners and managers, who, having signed on other Negro players, made "special arrangements" for them. A few managers, however, held out. They switched training sites from the South to the West. When hotels refused accommodations to Negro players, these managers changed hotels. Rather than bench Negro players in those states that had hastily passed laws enjoining integrated athletic contests, these managers refused to play at all. Gradually their defiance of Southern custom caught on, and gradually the South yielded. Moreover, Negro players were star attractions in the North and West. By 1952, opposition to them had collapsed, and by 1955, every major league team in the country, and most of the minor league teams based in the South, had a quota of Negro players.

Though Negroes admire and take pride in the accomplishments of their athletes and entertainers, they have a rather special regard for those Negro thinkers and writers (lately turned activists) who serve as emissaries from the black world to the white. Serious Negro writers have always felt, and have been encouraged by their people to feel, that their deepest commitment is to the race situation in America. Negro writers—including poets, playwrights and novelists—consider themselves spokesmen for their people. In the 1940's and '50's, the best of them were speaking more clearly and were listened to more attentively than ever before.

Richard Wright was one of the first of these, but Wright moved permanently to France in 1948, and lost touch with the living reality of America. Yet the audience that had listened to him in 1939, when *Uncle Tom's Children* was published, and in 1940, when *Native Son* came out, was still there, and had in fact grown larger. It was the audience that Gwendolyn Brooks attracted when she won the Pulitzer Prize for poetry in 1950. Though *Go Tell it on The Mountain,* his first novel, spoke loud and clear, James Baldwin was not really listened to until he published his first collection of essays, *Notes of a Native Son.* In 1953, Ralph Ellison won the National Book Award with his novel *Invisible Man,* which stayed on the best seller list for eight months. It was in the 1950's also that Langston Hughes, still the most durable American Negro writer, turned a series of prose folk pieces into a play, "Simply Heavenly", and Ossie Davis presented a biting satire, "Purlie Victorious" on Broadway. In 1960, Lorraine Hansberry's "A Raisin in the Sun" won the Critics Circle Award, the highest honor America bestows upon a play.

But it was the activists, the local leaders, and the ubiquitous "field workers" of the Congress of Racial Equality, the Student Non-Violent Coordinating Committee, the National Association for the Advancement of Colored People, and for Dr. Martin Luther King's Southern Christian Leadership Conference who were having the greatest impact. They were slowly effecting changes in social behavior and in political and economic practices. Some religious organizations—the Southern Baptists, the Presbyterians, and the Lutherans—that had formerly condoned segregation, now encouraged, at least half-heartedly, integration of various activities. Negroes were invited to policy-making boards such as presbyteries, home missions, and synods. Private church-related colleges and universities in the South, such as Duke, Vanderbilt, and Wake Forest began accepting Negro students, though only on a token basis. More meaningful to more people, however, were the changes in the political climate and in the commercial and industrial world, where pressure from the federal government was brought to bear. In Tennessee, Kentucky, and Georgia, where Negroes were beginning to fill the voter rolls, politicians eschewed racism and solicited Negro support. Industrial firms under contract to the federal government recruited Negro workers, trained them, upgraded them. "White Only" signs were less common than they used to be.

There was resistance to these changes, and some of it had unhappy consequences. In 1962, when the Governor of Mississippi marshalled all the power of the state to resist the court-ordered admission of a Negro to the state university, rioting followed, and two people were killed before federalized militia brought things under control. Medger Evers, a field worker for the NAACP, was killed from ambush. In 1962-63, more than a dozen bomb blasts rocked the Negro section of Birmingham, Alabama, and one of these took the lives of four Negro girls, the oldest of whom was just fourteen. In Mississippi, three civil rights workers—two of whom were white—were murdered. A Negro army reserve officer, returning from summer training, was gunned down by nightriders in Georgia. In Alabama, a white woman civil rights worker was shot to death by members of the Ku Klux Klan.

"Adequately and Fairly"

All such instances, however, seemed to win more people to the side of moderation. Many white Southern citizens who were not actively for civil rights were certainly opposed to violent resistance to them, and they responded to what President Kennedy called the "moral issue". "This is not a legal or legislative issue alone," he told a nation-wide television audience on June 11, 1963. "It is better to settle these matters in the courts than on the streets, and new laws are needed at every level. But law alone cannot make men see right . . . . We preach freedom around the world, and we mean it. And we cherish our freedom here at home. But are we to say to the world—and much more importantly to each other— that this is the land of the free, except for Negroes? That we have no second-class citizens, except Negroes? That we have no class or caste system, no ghettos, no master race, except with respect to Negroes?"

Even as the President spoke, the most far-reaching civil rights legislation ever proposed was on his desk for a final perusal. Earlier, he had issued two Executive Orders. One, 10935, guaranteed equality of opportunity in federal employment, and the other, 11063, banned discrimination in federally-financed housing; but these had merely scratched the surface of the problem. The new legislation dug deep. It outlawed discrimination in all state programs receiving federal aid, in all employment, in labor unions, and in places of public accommodation, and it permitted the Justice Department itself to bring suit to desegregate public schools and to safeguard voting rights. Eights days after his nation-wide television appearance, President Kennedy sent the bill to Congress.

Meanwhile, though, less publicized efforts in another direction were beginning to produce a more subtle result. For more than a century, Negro scholars and other professional intellectuals had tried to make traction in the mind of America, but to little avail. They had explored the "sociology" and the "psychology" of race, but their findings were generally ignored. What Negro historians had discovered about American history and the Negro's role in it had been discounted by all but Negroes themselves, and the image of the Negro as a nonentity, as an invisible and non-contributing member of the American society, was fixed in the average American mind. Even historians as reputable as James Truslow Adams, Charles and Mary Beard, Henry Steele Commager, and Samuel Eliot Morison had left this image undisturbed. But now, suddenly, almost as if acting in concert, several young white scholars and intellectuals began a new examination of American historical sources. Caught up in the current of unprecedented events, they looked into the past for some explanation of the present, and what they found contradicted nearly everything that most people had been taught to believe. They discovered that racial segregation in America was not a "long-standing tradition", but was of relatively recent date. They learned that the Negro's "crusade for freedom" had really started in the 1660's, when the Colonial Assembly of Virginia found it "manifested . . . that many negroes have lately beene, and are now out in rebellion in sundry parts of this country." They learned that free Negroes held conventions almost every year from 1726 to the eve of the Civil War, and that they protested everything from slavery to poll taxes and regularly petitioned for the redress of innumerable grievances.

These and other discoveries discredited many of the textbooks in common use in the public schools. Negroes had complained about these texts for years: they were biased; they showed no comprehension of the facts; either they left the Negro out altogether, or they included him in a derogatory fashion. Now the validity of these complaints had the backing of reputable scholars outside the race—of C. Vann Woodward, Kenneth Stampp, David Cronon, Wilson Record, Richard Bardolph. Here and there in the North, public school officials ordered a reappraisal of text books and curricula. Los Angeles had "a war of the textbooks". Public school officials in New York and Detroit commissioned the writing of texts that would "treat Negroes and other minorities adequately and fairly".

The criterion "adequately and fairly" was increasingly applied, too, by federal agencies, for the sensitivity to issues of equality and opportunity was sharpened by the positive attitude of the Kennedy-Johnson administration. A number of Negroes were brought into federal positions of great responsibility. A Negro was appointed one of three commissioners of the District of Columbia. The U. S. Office of Education, the National Science Foundation, and the Department of Health, Education and Welfare elevated Negroes to posts on the administrative and policy-making level. Thurgood Marshall, a distinguished civil rights lawyer and chief of the NAACP's Legal Defense, was named to the bench of the federal Second Court of Appeals. George L. P. Weaver was made Assistant Secretary of Labor, and Carl Rowan, who was later to be the Director of the U. S. Information Agency, was sent as Ambassador to Finland. Rowan was the fifth Negro to attain ambassadorial rank.

But the high level appointments of Negroes to city, state, and federal positions, and even to comparable jobs in the private sector of the power structure, scarcely touched the disabilities and inequities that plagued the masses of Negroes. They were poor and, by all statistical measurements, growing poorer. They had the poorest housing, the poorest schools, the poorest health. Though they comprised only ten percent of the labor force, they were twenty percent of the unemployed, and three times as many Negroes as whites were underemployed. From the end of World War II to 1963, the Federal government, through one or another of its agencies, had underwritten more than $115 billion for non-farm housing, but local housing authorities had the option of designating either open or segregated housing, and most had chosen the latter. Less than two percent of the new housing had been made available to Negroes. Ten years after the school desegregation decision, less than one percent of all Negro public school students in the South were getting the superior education presumably available to them in "white" schools.

Of course the Civil Rights Bill, which President Kennedy sent to Congress in the summer of 1963, was appreciated, but of what practical good was it to the masses of Negroes? It was a fine thing to outlaw discrimination in employment, in labor unions, and in state programs receiving Federal aid, but who would police the circumventions and bring the circumventers to book? Or what would stop the Southern states from refusing federal assistance altogether? And why did the Civil Rights Bill limit the Justice Department's mandate to bringing suits for school desegregation and to safeguard voting rights? Why not have the Justice Department bring suits against discriminating employers and labor unions?

In any case, for Negroes to be treated "adequately and fairly" was not enough. The gap between where they were, and where it was the intent of the bill for them to be, was too wide. Before they could be equal, they had first to catch up.

Whitney Young, Executive Secretary of the National Urban League, was one of the first to realize this and to suggest a solution to it. He proposed "preferential treatment" for Negroes. He urged "the responsible leadership of our country to undertake a massive 'Marshall Plan' approach of intensified special effort to close the wide economic, social and educational gap. . . . If those who make the decisions in this country are really sincere about closing the gaps, they must go further than fine impartiality. We [Negroes] must have, in fact, special consideration if we are to compensate for the scars left by three hundred years of deprivation." Young suggested that in situations where Negroes and whites were equally qualified—for jobs, for apprenticeship training, and scholarships, for admission to college, and for housing —Negroes be given preference. Though they employed such terms as "compensatory treatment", "phase programs", and "reverse quotas", other Negro leaders soon espoused the same idea.

The idea was neither new nor complicated. When it was first broached after the Civil War, the argument for it was that Negroes should be compensated for the "unrequited toil" of slavery. The argument seemed morally valid still, and as the head of the Urban League pointed out, it was supported by the obvious fact that to put Negroes in a race with runners (the whites) who have already "lapped the field" was to make it impossible for Negroes ever to catch up. First equalize—by following a policy of preferential treatment for as long as it takes to accomplish equalization— and then proceed.

But there were arguments against it, too. Preferential treatment is discrimination in reverse. Why should Negroes be given something no other American minority group has ever asked for, much less had? Today is not in hostage to yesterday. At the very time when the demand is to eliminate race as a factor, compensatory treatment, which would impose a penalty on white men, emphasizes it.

The arguments on both sides were heated.

Meanwhile, the traditional Negro organizations continued to protest the government's failure to implement those rights that a spate of laws—beginning with the 1954 school decision—had already granted to Negroes: the right to work in industries that held government contracts; the right to live on a desegregated basis in housing that had been constructed with the aid of federal funds; the right to travel in public carriers without being discriminated against. But there was a growing feeling that something more was needed to achieve the hoped-for results. In many places, where administrative delays and ingenious "legal" appeals did not thwart them altogether, the laws were complied with only grudgingly and in token fashion—though newspaper headlines continued to proclaim that all was well on the racial front. Some dramatic event was needed to call the whole country's attention to the true state of things. And in the summer of 1963, the dramatic event occurred.

Two hundred thousand Negroes and at least ten thousand whites (including fifteen U. S. senators) staged a March on Washington. The *New York Times* described it as "the greatest assembly for the redress of grievances the country had ever seen". It was peaceful, it was even happy—as when a long-scattered family comes together—but it was protest, and representatives of all the responsible institutions of the American society took part in it. There were labor groups and church groups, industry and commerce, educators and entertainers, Democrats and Republicans and Socialists. The March on Washington represented a "coalition of conscience" and that conscience spoke out loud and clear a few months later, when, in spite of the stubborn opposition of some die-hard Southerners, the sweeping Kennedy-Johnson Civil Rights Bill was passed by the Congress. On July 2, 1964, it was signed by President Johnson who had worked vigorously for its passage.

In time the new law would settle many things, and though the March on Washington probably helped to delay the development of a crisis phase in race relations, the Negro masses were impatient and restless. In the following fall and winter, and through the spring of 1965, signs of crisis began

to appear in unexpected places. In the North, where the
legal premises had always favored civil equality, and where
it was generally thought that political solutions were available to Negroes, the race problem, paradoxically, was more
complex than in the South. In the North, it was not simply
a matter of definable, intractable prejudice. The problem
was less literal, much harder to define. It was signified in
such phrases as "racial imbalance", "de facto segregation",
"the ghetto mind". Moreover, in the North there was no
way to singularize the instruments and authorities that gen-
erated and controlled social change. The "enemy" was
ubiquitous shadow.

It was perhaps as much for this as for any other reason
that Negro demonstrations in the North were more spon-
taneous, fanatical, and militant, and less focused than in
the South. Demonstrations in the North took the form of
school boycotts, "lie-ins" and garbage-dumpings in the
streets to block traffic. In San Francisco, demonstrators
crowded into supermarkets, filled shopping carts with commodities and left them at the check-out counters. They went
into restaurants, ordered elaborate meals and left them un-
touched and unpaid for. They picketed automobile sales-
rooms, and banks, and, on one occasion, laid all-night seige
to a hotel. Their grievances did not center in these establishments. The establishments were surrogates for the enemy.

These outbreaks of civil disobedience reached a climax in
the Negro ghetto in New York on July 18, 1964, less than
three weeks after the passage of the Civil Rights Bill. At a
street ralley in Harlem on the evening of the 18th, a teen-
age girl, representing the Congress of Racial Equality, reminded her audience that an off-duty, white policeman had
shot and killed a fifteen year old Negro boy two days before.
"James Powell was shot because he was black", the girl said.
Apparently that was enough to set off an unexpected out-

break of violence, in which Negroes vented their nameless
anger against the "white man"—his person, his property, his
power. Though there were no known deaths in the tumult,
the riot raged for several hours and resulted in damages of
several million dollars. Two years later, similar circumstances produced more tragic results in the Los Angeles
community of Watts.

But things other than the death of a Negro boy at the
hands of a white policeman contributed to the Negroes' emotional outburst that night in New York. A national election
campaign was building toward its height. George Wallace,
the governor of Alabama, had entered three Northern state
presidential primaries, and, preaching racism under the
guise of "states' rights", won thirty percent of the votes in
Wisconsin and Indiana, and nearly fifty percent in Maryland. He raised the "terrible prospect of race as a political
issue in a national campaign". And when Barry Goldwater
disregarded the Republican Party's will to moderation and
began wooing the Southern vote, also under the guise of
"states' rights", no one was deceived, and Goldwater suf-
fered one of the most humiliating defeats ever inflicted on a
candidate.

For states' rights both in theory and in practice had been
more illusory than real for thirty years. The corollary to states'
rights is states' responsibilities, and during the depression
of the 1930's, the states—and especially the poorer states in
the South—were glad to delegate to the federal government
the responsibility for economic rehabilitation, for the building and repair of roads and bridges, dams and levees, and
other public works. This delegation of responsibility had
continued and spread, until by 1964, there were literally
dozens of federal grant-in-aid programs for the states—in education and agriculture, in power plants and conservation of
resources, and in welfare and medical care—as well as programs that called for outright federal assistance. In the final

analysis, the ultimate protection of privileges and property, of life and liberty rests with the federal government, while the power to make civil and criminal laws remains with the states.

It was this power that some of the Southern states used in an effort to contravene federal law. They used it to persecute those who tried to exercise their federally guaranteed rights. In 1964-65, hundreds of Negroes and white civil rights workers were jailed under one or another hastily-erected state or local law. Burke Marshall, chief of the Civil Rights Division of the Justice Department, declared that "our basic assumptions about the workings of justice in state courts are wrong. . . . Examples of abuse are compounded by. . . other evidence of the weight of state authority thrusting imbalance into the processes of justice where racial customs are threatened."

It was this "thrusting imbalance" that the federal government now undertook to correct. Throughout 1964-65, the President's Civil Rights Commission went into various states to hold hearings on the denial of equal protection of the laws. The Justice Department initiated suits against private conspiracies and public ("official") acts that "legally" deprived individuals of their civil rights. It moved against the discrimination in public education and public accommodations. It obtained federal injunctions to keep states from prosecuting citizens who, in trying to exercise their rights, were charged with "disorderly conduct", "refusal to obey an officer", and "failing to heed a traffic sign". The Justice Department sent federal officers into the South to by-pass state laws designed to frustrate or slow down the voting registration of Negroes. On the grounds that private enterprises were in fact "public" if there was state involvement, or if they had a "community character", the Supreme Court dismissed hundreds of suits of trespass some of the Southern states had brought against people who took part in sit-ins.

President Johnson appointed a Council on Equal Opportunity, in 1965, and made Vice-President Hubert H. Humphrey, its chairman. And in the summer of that same year, the federal government launched its campaign against poverty, ignorance, and unemployment among Negroes and whites. It launched the Head Start program, and Upward Bound, and the Rural Task Force and VISTA—a concert of programs designed to reach down into the masses, black and white, who are as yet incapable of coping with the abstract idea of civil rights, but who can benefit from the practical application of them.

In 1967, the old dogmas seem to be in discard. No thoughtful American would say that the millenium is in sight, but neither could he deny that a great mobilization of national purpose is under way, or that already there are auguries of a future that cannot come too soon. President Johnson, in his State-of-the-Union speech, epitomized the will and leadership of a people who are inexorably committed to the abolition of inequities at home. This commitment is not only a matter of right and moral obligation, but it is a matter of necessity for a nation that is, in so many ways, a model for the rest of the world.

Suggestions for Further Reading

Baldwin, James, *The Fire Next Time*. Dial Press, New York, 1963; Dell, New York.*
A personal essay brilliantly written and effectively representing the thought and the temper of the Negro people since the 1950's.

Buckmaster, Henrietta, *Let My People Go*. Peter Smith, Magnolia, Massachusetts, 1959; Beacon Press, Boston.*
The dramatic story of the first privately organized bi-racial struggle against slavery. It covers the whole period from the last decades of the eighteenth century to the eve of the Civil War.

Butcher, Margaret Just, *The Negro in American Culture*. Alfred A. Knopf, New York, 1956.
A critical analysis of the Negro's contributions to American culture.

Elkins, Stanley M., *Slavery, A Problem in American Intellectual and Institutional Life*. University of Chicago, Chicago, 1959; Grossett & Dunlap, New York, 1963.*
An historical account of the influence of slavery on the thought and the institutions in American life. It examines the development of racial ideas in the law and the operations of government in religion, in economics, and in society.

Franklin, John Hope, *From Slavery to Freedom*. Alfred A. Knopf, New York (revised edition), 1961.
A comprehensive, scholarly account of the influence of Negro slavery and freedom. The author begins with slavery in Africa, touches upon the European slave trade, but concentrates on slavery and its aftermath in America.

Franklin, John Hope, *Reconstruction After the Civil War*. University of Chicago Press, Chicago, 1961.*
An objective examination of the period, 1865-1878, immediately following the Civil War—the most misunderstood and misinterpreted era in American history. The book demolishes

* Books available in paperbound editions.

91

once and for all the myth of the Negro's responsibility for the "tragedy" of the times.

Franklin, John Hope, *The Emancipation Proclamation.* Doubleday, New York, 1963.*

A study of the factors that led to the writing of the Proclamation. Written in terms of the problems President Lincoln wrestled with, the book is a perceptive exploration of Lincoln's political and social thought.

Garfinkel, Herbert, *When Negroes March.* Free Press, Glencoe, Illinois, 1959.

A study of Negro techniques of protest and of the people who join them.

Greenberg, Jack, *Race Relations and American Law.* Columbia University Press, New York, 1959.

Since the Civil War, Negroes have used the law and the courts as battlegrounds for freedom and equality. The book is an account of that struggle.

Kennedy, Louise V., *The Negro Peasant Turns Cityward.* Columbia University Press, New York, 1930.

The urbanization of the Negro from the post-Civil War period to the great Negro migration of the first World War.

King, Martin Luther, *Stride Toward Freedom.* Harper & Row, New York, 1958.*

A study of the idea of non-violent resistance, and how Dr. King and his followers applied it in Montgomery, Alabama, in 1955.

Litwack, Leon F., *North of Slavery.* University of Chicago Press, Chicago, 1961.*

Valuable for its examination of the social and political thought in the North during slavery.

Locke, Alain, ed., *The New Negro: An Interpretation.* A & C Boni, New York, 1925.

This volume, part anthology, part history, contrasts the image of the "old" Negro—his compromising humility and patience, his estrangement from the general American society, his escape into his own social institutions, etc.—with the "new" Negro—his new-found self-respect, his determination to fight for his rights, etc.

* Books available in paperbound editions.

Logan, Rayford W., *The Negro in American Life and Thought: The Nadir, 1877-1901.* Dial Press, New York, 1954; Collier, New York, 1965.*
>The end of Reconstruction in 1877 saw the Negro reduced in civil and legal status almost to a condition of slavery. This book examines the period.

Lomax, Louis E., *The Negro Revolt.* Harper & Row, New York, 1962; New American Library, New York.*
>A journalistic account of what has been happening on the racial front from the time of the Supreme Court decision on school integration in 1954 to mid-1961.

Mannix, Daniel P., and Malcolm Cowley, *Black Cargoes: A History of the Atlantic Slave Trade, 1518-1865.* Viking Press, New York, 1962.*
>This book tells the story of the slave trade in terms of some of the chief personalities who plied it.

Meier, August, *Negro Thought in America: 1880-1915.* University of Michigan Press, Ann Arbor, Michigan, 1963.
>Principally concerned with such commanding figures of Negro thought and policy as Frederick Douglas, Booker T. Washington, W.E.B. DuBois, and the like, Meier's book is as careful an analysis of Negro intellectual (non-academic) leadership as one can hope to find.

Myrdal, Gunnar, *An American Dilemma.* Harper & Row, New York (revised edition), 1962; McGraw-Hill, New York.*
>Written by a Swedish sociologist, this is the classic study of racial interaction in America.

Nichols, Lee, *Breakthrough on the Color Front.* Random House, New York, 1954.
>In 1952, President Truman ordered the desegregation of the armed forces. This book tells how the order was carried out, and with what consequence.

Quarles, Benjamin, *Lincoln and the Negro.* Oxford University Press, New York, 1962.
>What were President Lincoln's thoughts on Negro slavery and freedom? What did he think of Negroes? What kind of future did he project for them? What action did he take,

* Books available in paperbound editions.

or fail to take, in their behalf? Quarles' book explores these questions.

Redding, Saunders, *On Being a Negro in America.* Bobbs-Merrill, New York, 1962; Bantam, New York, 1964.*
Personal essays on the Negro condition in America during the seminal twenty-five years from 1925 to 1950.

Redding, Saunders, *The Lonesome Road.* Doubleday, New York, 1958.*
The history of the Negro in America told in terms of the personalities who have dominated it.

Stampp, Kenneth M., *The Peculiar Institution.* Alfred A. Knopf, New York, 1956; Vintage, New York.*
Based on long-neglected source materials, this book is a perceptive reevaluation of slavery in America.

Woodward, C. Vann, *Origins of the New South, 1817-1913.* Louisiana State University Press, Baton Rouge, Louisiana, 1951.*
A valuable historical study of the South that emerged at the end of the Reconstruction Period.

* Books available in paperbound editions.

Index

abolitionists, 11, 13, 17, 20
Addams, Jane, 39, 42
AFL, *see* American Federation of Labor
Afro-American, 37
Air Force, U.S., 61
Alabama, 69, 70, 72, 73, 79, 87
Alexander, W.W., 42, 56
"All God's Chillun Got Wings", 53
American Colonization Society, 16
American Dilemma, An, 51
American Federation of Labor (AFL), 58
American Missionary Association, 32
American Missionary Society, 20
American Negro Labor Congress, 50
American Revolution, 9, 11, 13
Anderson, Marian, 77
Anderson, Sherwood, 53
Anglicans, 11; *see also* Episcopal Church
anti-lynching legislation, 40, 50
anti-slavery, *see* abolitionists
Antioch College, 72
Arkansas, 13, 69
Armstrong, Louis, 77
Armstrong, Samuel Chapman, 33
Army, U.S., 43-44, 62
Association for the Study of Negro Life and History, 50
Association of Southern Women for the Prevention of Lynching, 50
Atlanta, 32, 34, 41, 50, 58
Atlanta Baptist College, 33
Atlanta Exposition of 1895, 34
Attorney General, U.S., 64

Back-to-Africa movement, 49, 75
Baker, Josephine, 52
Baldwin, James, 78
Baptist Home Mission Society, 32
Baptists, 11
Baptists, Southern, 79
Bardolph, Richard, 82
Batuola, 53
Belafonte, Harry, 77
Bilbo, Theodore, 41
Black Codes, 7, 26
Black Dispatch, 37
Black Muslims, 75
Blaine, James G., 28
Boston, 50
Brooks, Gwendolyn, 78
Brotherhood of Sleeping Car Porters, 60
Brown, John, 16, 17
Brown, William Wells, 17
Bunche, Ralph, 56

Calhoun, John C., 15
Cane, 52
Carnegie, Andrew, 33
Catholics, 11, 55
Cato, 5
Charleston, South Carolina, 14, 32
Chesnutt, Charles W., 37
Chicago, 31, 37, 41, 48, 50, 53, 58
CIO, *see* Congress of Industrial Organizations
civil rights, 70-75, 78-80
civil rights bills, 27, 73, 83, 85, 86
Civil War, the, 18, 19-22, 81, 84

Civilian Conservation Corps (CCC), 56
Clay, Henry, 15
Colored Housewives League, 50
Commerce, U. S. Department of, 57
commercial exploitation of Negroes, 53-54
Commission on Civil Rights, 75, 88
Commission on Interracial Cooperation, 50
Committee on Civil Rights, 64
Committee on Fair Employment Practices, 61
Communism (Bolshevism), 47, 48, 49
Confederate States of America, 17-18, 19, 20, 21, 22, 30
Congress, U.S., v, 21, 28, 48, 56, 83
Congress of Industrial Organizations (CIO), 58
Congress of Racial Equality, *see* CORE
Connor, Eugene "Bull", 71
Constitution, U.S., 64, 65
Constitution, the Atlanta, 41, 50
Constitutional Convention of 1787, 11-12
CORE, 60, 72, 78, 86
cotton, 12, 13, 40
cotton gin, 13
Crisis, The, 39
Cronon, David, 82
Cullen, Countee, 52

Dark Laughter, 53
Darrow, Clarence, 50
Davis, Jefferson, 20, 28
Davis, Ossie, 78
Davis, Sammy Jr., 59
"de facto segregation", 86

Debs, Eugene V., 47
Declaration of Independence, 9
"Deep Are the Roots", 76
Defender, the Chicago, 37
Delaware, 19, 29
Democrats, 29, 39, 55, 56, 75, 85
Detroit, 63, 82
Dewey, John, 38
Dilliard, J.H., 42
discrimination, 31, 61, 73, 80, 85
District of Columbia, 21; *see also* Washington, D.C.
Douglas, Stephen A., 15, 16
Douglass, Frederick, 15, 17, 25
Dred Scott decision, 16
DuBois, W.E.B., 34-35, 37, 38, 39, 44
Duke University, 79

Eisenhower, Dwight D., 64, 70
Eleazer, Robert, 42
Ellington, Duke, 51, 77
Ellison, Ralph, 78
emancipation, 25; *see also* enfranchisement
Emancipation Proclamation, 19
"Emperor Jones, The", 53
enfranchisement, 25, 26, 29, 30
Episcopal Church, 11, 32-33; *see also* Anglicans
Evers, Medger, 79
Executive Order 8802, 61
Executive Order 10935, 80
Executive Order 11063, 80

Fair Employment Practices Act, 64
Fair Employment Practices Commission, 63
Farm Security Administration (FSA), 56

Faubus, Orville, 69
Fauset, Jessie, 52
Fifteenth Amendment, 28, 39
Fire in the Flint, 52
Fisher, Rudolph, 52
Fisk University, 33
Fitzgerald, Ella, 77
Florida, 3, 5, 55, 73
Forrest, Gen. Nathan Bedford, 21
Fort Sumter, 18
"four freedoms", 63
Fourteenth Amendment, 27, 65
Frankfurter, Felix, 39
Franklin, Benjamin, 11-12
Frazier, Franklin, 51
free Negroes, 13, 14, 25, 31
Freedmen's Bureau, 26, 27
Freedmen's Hospital, 38
"freedom rides", 72
Friends of Negro Freedom, 50
FSA, *see* Farm Security Administration
Fugitive Slave Law, 17

Garrison, William Lloyd, 15, 16
Garvey, Marcus, 49, 75
Georgia, 5, 9, 11, 13, 50, 58, 69, 73, 79
Gershwin, George, 53
ghetto, 41, 53, 62, 80, 86
Go Tell It on the Mountain, 78
Goldwater, Barry, 75, 87
"Grandfather Clauses", 39
Green, Paul, 53

Hampton Institute, 33
Hansberry, Lorraine, 78
Harding, Warren G., 47
Harlem, 53, 58-59, 86
Harper, Chancellor, 14
Harvard University, 58

Hastie, William, 56-57
Hayes, Rutherford B., 30
Hayne, Robert Y., 15
Hays, Arthur Garfield, 50
"head rights", 3
Head Start Program, 89
Henry, Patrick, 7
Herskovits, Melville T., 51
Heyward, DuBose, 53
Higginson, Col. Thomas Wentworth, 21
"Home of the Brave", 76
Home Owners Loan Corporation, 56
Homer Phillips Hospital, 38
Hoover, Herbert, 55
Horne, Lena, 59, 77
House Behind the Cedars, The, 37
Howard University, 74
Hughes, Langston, 52, 78
Humphrey, Hubert H., 89
Huntington, Collis, 33

Illinois, 32, 43, 56, 58
immigration, European, 14, 31, 40
"In Abraham's Bosom", 53
indentureship, 3
Indiana, 21, 87
industrial revolution, 12-13
integration, 61-62, 70, 79
Interior, U.S. Department of, 57
International Workers of the World, *see* IWW
"Intruder in the Dust", 76
Invisible Man, 78
IWW, 47, 48

Jackson, Andrew, 15
Jayhawkers, 29

jazz, 51, 54
Jeanes Fund, Anna T., 42
Jefferson, Thomas, 4, 5, 7, 16
Jobs-for-Negroes campaign, 58
Johnson, Andrew, 15
Johnson, Charles S., 51
Johnson, Guy B., 51
Johnson, Lyndon B., 82, 85, 89
Justice, U.S. Department of, 48, 80, 83, 88

Kansas, 16, 32
Kennedy, John F., 75, 80, 82, 83, 85
Kentucky, 19, 55, 79
King, Dr. Martin Luther Jr., 71, 79
Knights of the White Camelia, 29
Ku Klux Klan, 29, 47, 69, 70, 80

Labor, U.S. Department of, 42
La Follette, Robert M., 47
Laurens, Henry, 7
Legal Defense Fund, 70, 82
Lewis, John L., 58
Liberator, The, 16
Liberia, 16
Lincoln, Abraham, 15, 16, 17, 18, 19, 22, 25, 26, 30
literacy tests, 30
Little Rock, Arkansas, 69
Locke, Alain, 51
Locke, John, 4
Los Angeles, 62, 82
"Lost Boundaries", 76
Louis, Joe, 77
Louisiana, 13, 28, 69, 71, 73
Lunceford, Jimmie, 51
Lutherans, 79
lynchings, 43, 47

Mamba's Daughters, 53
manumission, 16-17
Maran, Réné, 53
March on Washington, 85
Marine Corps, U.S., 61
Marshall, Burke, 88
Marshall, Thurgood, 82
Maryland, 5, 19, 56, 87
Mason, George, 11
McKay, Claude, 52
Meharry Medical College, 74
Mercy Hospital, 37
Methodists, 11
Michigan, 63
migration, wartime, 62
Miller, Kelly, 37
Mississippi, 27, 41, 69, 73, 79
Missouri, 16, 19
Missouri Compromise, 16
Mitchell, Arthur W., 56
Monroe, James, 16
Montgomery, Alabama, 72
Morton, Ferdinand Q., 55
Moton, Robert R., 43
Myrdal, Gunnar, 51

NAACP (National Association for the Advancement of Colored People), 38-39, 42, 50, 60, 64, 65, 70, 72, 78, 79, 82
National Freedmen's Relief Association, 20
National Industrial Recovery Act, 56
National Urban League, *see* Urban League, National
National Youth Administration (NYA), 56
Native Son, 78
Navy, U.S., 61
Nebraska, 48
Negro artists, 53
Negro athletes, 77

Negro church, 32
Negro education, 60, 74, 79
Negro employment, 31, 60, 61, 74
Negro entertainers, 51-52, 59, 77
Negro farmers, 31, 40, 57
Negro History Week, 59
Negro housing, 57, 60, 83, 85
Negro newspapers, 37
Negro poverty, 82-83
"Negro Renaissance", 53
Negro "revolution", 74-79
Negro soldiers, 9, 20, 21, 22, 43-44, 61-62
Negro urban life, 41; *see also* ghetto
Negro writers, 52-53, 78
Negroes and politics, 27, 28, 29, 55-56
"New Deal", 56
New Orleans, 14, 32, 53
"New" Negroes, 48, 49-51, 69, 76
New York City, 5, 13, 50, 53, 58-59, 82, 86, 87
New York State, 55, 56
New York Times, The, 56, 85
New York University, 58
Niagara declaration, 34-35
Nigger Heaven, 53
Nixon, Richard M., 75
non-violence, 71-73, 86
North Carolina, 4, 5, 6, 27, 28, 55
Northwestern University, 51
Not Without Laughter, 52
Notes of a Native Son, 78

Odum, Howard, 50-51
Ohio, 32, 72
Oklahoma, 32
O'Neal, Frederick, 77
O'Neill, Eugene, 53

Oregon, 62
Otis, James, 4
Ovington, Mary, 39
Owens, Jesse, 77

Paine, Thomas, 4
Packinghouse Workers, 58
Park, Robert, 51
Parker, John J., 55
Peabody, George, 33
Pennsylvania, 4, 11, 21, 32, 48, 56
Pennsylvania Society for the Abolition of Slavery, 11
Perez, Leander, H., 71
Pershing, Gen. John J., 44
Peterkin, Julia, 53
Philadelphia, 13-14, 37-38, 50
Phillips, Wendell, 15
picketing, 73, 86
Plessy v. Ferguson, 30
poll tax, 30
"Porgy and Bess", 53
Portland, Oregon, 62, 63
"preferential treatment", 83-84
Presbyterian Board, 32
Presbyterians, 4, 79
Price, Leontyne, 77
Progressives, 55
Provident Hospital, 37
"Purlie Victorious", 78

Quakers, 4, 8, 11

Race Adjustment, 37
racial commissions, 50, 51
"racial imbalance", 86
"racial inequality", 33
Radical Republicans, 26-27

"Raisin in the Sun, A", 78
Randolph-Macon College, 15
Reconstruction, 25-35, 39, 42
Record, Wilson, 82
Red Cross, 43, 44
Republicans, 17, 21, 26-27, 29, 39, 55, 56, 75, 85, 87
"return to normalcy", 47-54
Revels, Hiram, 28
"Rhapsody in Blue", 53
Rhode Island, 13
riots, 43, 48, 59
Robinson, "Bojangles", 51
Robinson, Jackie, 77
Robinson, Sugar Ray, 77
Rockefeller, John D., 33
Roosevelt, Franklin D., 56, 61, 63
Roosevelt, Mrs. Eleanor, 61
Rosenwald, Julius, 42
Rowan, Carl, 82
runaway slaves, 5-6, 9, 16, 17
Rural Task Force, 89

San Francisco, 62, 63, 86
Sands, Diana, 77
Savannah, Georgia, 32
Scarlet Sister Mary, 53
"second-class citizenship", 33, 80
segregation, 30, 31, 40, 41, 43, 57, 65, 73, 77, 81, 86
"separate but equal", 30, 65
"Simply Heavenly", 78
sit-ins, 72
Slater, John F., 33
Slater, Samuel, 12
slave rebellions, 5-6, 12
slavery, 3-4, 5, 6-8, 12, 13, 14-18, 19, 84
slaves, free, *see* free Negroes
Smalls, Robert, 28
Smith, Alfred E., 55
Smith, Bessie and Mamie, 51

Smith, Dr. William A., 15
Society for the Propagation of the Gospel, 8
Souls of Black Folk, The, 37
South Carolina, 4, 5, 7, 9, 14, 21, 27, 28, 48, 65
Southern Christian Leadership Conference (SCLC), 79
"Southern Manifesto", 74
Southern Youth Congress, 60
Spingarn, Arthur, 39, 42
Stampp, Kenneth, 82
State, U.S. Department of, 57, 63
states' rights, 12, 15, 31-32, 69, 87
Steel Workers, 58
Stevens, Thaddeus, 27, 30
Storey, Moorfield, 38
Student Non-Violent Coordinating Committee (SNCC), 72, 78
Sumner, Charles, 15, 27, 30
Supreme Court, U.S., 16, 30, 55, 57, 64-65, 69, 72, 88

Talladega College, 33
Tennessee, 55, 72, 79
Texas, 32, 48, 55
Thurman, Wallace, 52
Toomers, Jean, 52
Truman, Harry S., 63, 64
Tuskegee Institute, 33, 43

Uncle Tom's Cabin, 16
Uncle Tom's Children, 78
United Auto Workers, 58
United Colored Democracy, 55
United Mine Workers, 58
United Nations, v, 63, 64, 75, 76
Universal Negro Improvement Association, 49

University of Chicago, 51, 58
University of North Carolina, 51
University of Texas, 65
Upward Bound, 89
Urban League, National, 38-39,
    42, 50, 58, 60, 72, 83-84
U.S. v. Cruikshank, 30

Van Vechten, Carl, 53
Vanderbilt University, 72, 79
Villard, Oswald G., 38
Virginia, 3, 4, 5, 7, 9, 11, 55, 69,
    81
VISTA, 89
Wade-Davis Bill, 26

Wages and Hours Bill, 57
Wake Forest College, 79
Wallace, George, 87
Walling, William English, 38-39
Washington, Booker T., 33-35,
    37, 43
Washington, D.C., 21, 28, 38,
    40, 48, 50

Washington, George, 9
Washington, March on, 85
Waters, Ethel, 51
Watts district, 87
Ways of White Folks, The, 52
Weaver, George L.P., 82
Weaver, Robert, 57
Webster, Daniel, 15
West Virginia, 56
White Citizens Council, 69
White, George, H., 28
White, Walter, 52
Whitney, Eli, 13
Williams, Aubrey, 56
Williams, Dr. Daniel Hale, 38
Wilson, Woodrow, 39-40, 43
Woodward, C. Vann, 28, 82
Works Progress Administration
    (WPA), 57
World War I, 42-44
World War II, 60, 61, 74, 76
Wright, Richard, 78

YMCA, 43
Young, Whitney, 83